# MAKING CHANGES EASILY

## The Change Guide for People in Business

**LOUISE CORICA**

Copyright © 2014 Louise Corica.

All rights reserved. No part of this book may be used or reproduced by any means, graphic, electronic, or mechanical, including photocopying, recording, taping or by any information storage retrieval system without the written permission of the publisher except in the case of brief quotations embodied in critical articles and reviews.

Balboa Press books may be ordered through booksellers or by contacting:

Balboa Press
A Division of Hay House
1663 Liberty Drive
Bloomington, IN 47403
www.balboapress.com.au
1 (877) 407-4847

Because of the dynamic nature of the Internet, any web addresses or links contained in this book may have changed since publication and may no longer be valid. The views expressed in this work are solely those of the author and do not necessarily reflect the views of the publisher, and the publisher hereby disclaims any responsibility for them.

The author of this book does not dispense medical advice or prescribe the use of any technique as a form of treatment for physical, emotional, or medical problems without the advice of a physician, either directly or indirectly. The intent of the author is only to offer information of a general nature to help you in your quest for emotional and spiritual well-being. In the event you use any of the information in this book for yourself, which is your constitutional right, the author and the publisher assume no responsibility for your actions.

Any people depicted in stock imagery provided by Thinkstock are models, and such images are being used for illustrative purposes only. Certain stock imagery © Thinkstock.

Printed in the United States of America.

ISBN: 978-1-4525-2417-7 (sc)
ISBN: 978-1-4525-2418-4 (e)

Balboa Press rev. date: 05/20/2014

This book is dedicated to my parents for providing a living example of a good work ethic and teaching me the importance of never giving up if I don't first succeed; to my brothers and sisters for their shared experiences in business and contributions when a second opinion was needed; to my grandparents, great aunts and uncles, and aunts and uncles, who gave an added dimension to my life lessons over the years; to close friends Pop, Jan, and Mary for their continued and ongoing encouragement and support through some really tough times over the years. I send best wishes to my nieces and nephews as they grow and make changes in their own lives. I am grateful to be blessed with sight to see the sunrise, hearing to enjoy the sound of the birds as they sing so joyously at the dawn of every new day, and feeling to experience the freshness of the morning air. These are the gifts I value most each day I am here. Smile today and be glad that you have this moment in time. The lyrics from Pharrell Williams song, "Happy," "Sunshine she's here, you can take a break," are apt because it's what my days are like now. You, too, can clap along if you know what happiness is for you. Now, that's the truth!

You cannot teach a man anything; you can only help him find it within himself.

—Galileo Galilei

# CONTENTS

Foreword .................................................................. xi
Preface ................................................................... xv
Acknowledgements ................................................ xix
Introduction........................................................... xxi

Chapter 1   Know What Change Is............................. 1
Chapter 2   Develop Your Vision of Your
            Change Ideas.......................................20
Chapter 3   Brainstorm Change Ideas and
            Workshop the Best Ideas ..................... 48
Chapter 4   Motivation and
            Commitment to Change .......................63
Chapter 5   Change How Your Business
            Thinks—Step by Step ..........................76
Chapter 6   Principles for Planning
            Change—Just the Basics ....................106
Chapter 7   Essential Change Management
            Practices and Rules........................... 139
Chapter 8   Techniques and Tips........................... 157
Chapter 9   Change and Productivity ....................168
Chapter 10  Putting It All Together ........................ 178

Appendix................................................................203

# FOREWORD

Adapting to a sudden, unexpected change in our personal or business lives is one of the most difficult challenges in life. It' a natural reaction to want to have full control over our lives and seek out ways to make everything as it was. But the truth is no matter how hard we try there are always going to be situations in our lives that we have no control over. As the saying goes – The only constant in life is change. Change is positive, it brings opportunities to expand both personally and professionally and with almost every new life experience there are both advantages and disadvantages. At first glance you might not appreciate all of the aspects of a change you are facing but by drilling down into a situation you are certain to find aspects that you do love.

So what happens for those who choose to avoid the constant flow of changes that go hand in hand with being a human? In our life's journey we have all come across those who seem to spend most of their time hiding from the wonderful opportunities that life offers. Shackled by a lack of self-confidence and fearful of what each day will bring they constantly sabotage their chance to ever reach their full potential by not adapting to change. No one has ever reached their full potential by playing it safe and docking close to harbor in an effort to avoid waves rocking their life boat. In actual fact intensely focusing on ensuring everything stays static opposed to stretching yourself to accommodate and reach new goals as circumstances change uses more energy. The truth is there is only one place where we encounter complete stillness and unfortunately that's after we take our last breath.

So is there a magic formula or hidden secret to managing change, are their methods you can take on board to become more adaptable and efficient so that you are always poised and ready and able to face change head and come out the other end triumphant? If you've spent years wrestling with an avoidance attitude towards managing change the good news if you can now put that issue to rest because within the pages of this insightful book you'll discover just how manageable change is when you have the right resources, knowledge and tools at your disposal.

If you want to become your best-self, embrace life and squeeze all of the opportunities available for you to grow personally and professional you have to accept change for what it is. For many people change is framed with negative connotations, but when you accept change, you'll find it's the catalyst that provides you with a clean slate on which your future plans, self -confidence, education and flexibility is built.

Through the pages of this book, self- education, repositioning your attitude and embracing change for all it offers your life will be enriched. In the end all it takes is a 'can do' mind-set and the drive and passion to believe in your own ability so you can harness all that you are destined to achieve.

## **END**

For further information contact:
Lynette L Palmen AM
Founder and Managing Director
Women's Network Australia
www.womensnetwork.com.au

# PREFACE

We all experience the challenge of change from time to time. This book will help you manage change more easily.

There is a reason I wrote this book. I started off with few advantages, but I have an inner strength, tenacity, and staying power that have surprised even me at times. A near-death experience in high school changed my life for the better. When I was training for the state championships in discus, shot put, and javelin during my final year of school, an illness incapacitated me to the point at which I had to learn how to speak and walk again. Speech therapy, physio, and numerous tests became the daily norm for me for several years. The plans I had had for my life and career were gone, and I had to rethink everything about my life and what I could do and make new plans. As it happened, having to push through the pain of recovery and the uncertainty of what lay ahead made me even more determined and stronger for the experience.

I worked full time and studied at night to earn a Bachelor of Laws degree, a Diploma of Legal Practice, a Diploma of Risk Management and Business Continuity, a Diploma of Linguistics (Basic), Certificate IV in Training and Assessment, and Certificates in Project Management, Leadership and Management, Time Management and Basic Supervision, to name a few. The work I did in all of these disciplines provided a great foundation for all the roles I have undertaken. There is always more to learn.

My illness made me work harder; whether in school, sports, further education, or as an employee, I wanted to be the best I could be. I worked multiple jobs to earn the money I needed for my education, as learning was and is a passion. I studied on my own time, as many disciplines as my budget would allow. These experiences made me push harder when others might have given up or wanted someone else to pay their way. The people I have met since then, who had far greater challenges than my own, inspired and motivated me to aim for even bigger things. My approach to working on projects with an *attitude of gratitude* and a positive outlook has put me in touch with many outstanding businessmen and businesswomen, most of whom inspired me to do even greater things with the time I am given.

Change is inevitable. Some people accept change, and others resist it. Coming from a rural background and having a passion for sports and learning have developed in me a drive to succeed and to be the best I can be in whatever I do.

Throughout my career I have noticed that keeping things simple is the best approach. Working in the fast-paced mining industry for several years, where the operations are open 24/7, and everyone has to play their part and do it well to avoid negative consequences taught me the value of well-laid plans and that, when you play your role effectively, everyone wins. Your ability to do what counts, to achieve the changes you hope for, and to do just that bit more each time is the key.

The methods, techniques and concepts in the chapters that follow are practical. There are footnotes and citations for the documented evidence and survey results, but the focus isn't on academic detail. The ten ways to make changes easily are the most important elements—the supportive tips to help you make a start in your own life and business.

You are where you are because of past decisions and activities, but you can achieve great things with the simplest of changes. If you challenge yourself to change one thing, even this course correction can see you on a different shore than you could have ever imagined.

You are in charge of your destiny, whether it's your day-to-day activities or a lifelong passion yet unfulfilled.

> Forbes' thought of the day: "The only thing constant in life is change." — Francois de La Rochefoucauld

# ACKNOWLEDGEMENTS

My thanks to Lynette Palmen, AM, Founder and Managing Director of Women's Network Australia, for her ability to inspire her business members. I appreciated the assistance of the businesswomen who provided quotations and words of wisdom from their business experiences for my first book.

I am also grateful for a few of my *stand-out* bosses who challenged me in the past two decades: the late Barry Whitehead, studio manager at my first job, who showed me how creativity sells. Geoff Price, general manager of operations at my first mining job, who challenged me more than any other boss to *learn it all* in whatever role I was in. Roy Swan, technical director in my second mining role, who showed me that, with an extra bit of polish, one could shine even in a dusty environment.

My thanks to Ms Quentin Bryce, a governor of Australia, whom I met when she was governor of Queensland, who inspired me at our first meeting with her encouraging words to keep working toward my goals and challenged me to shape my own destiny.

I also thank the Australian Institute of Company Directors, which offered the scholarship I won for young women who aspire to be executives and for directorship placement.

Finally, I am sincerely grateful to the teams at Balboa Press for working with me, sharing their specialised skills and talents, providing sound critique, and encouraging me to finish what I started.

Over the past several years, certain events have motivated me to make some hard decisions and bring about big changes in my life. The challenge was to make these decisions and all the necessary changes to live my dreams.

# INTRODUCTION

> Far away there in the sunshine are my highest aspirations. I may not reach them, but I can look up and see their beauty, believe in them and try to follow where they lead. —Louisa May Alcott

Ever since I was young, I have wanted to be in business. I was surrounded by the family businesses. I loved to write, and with the encouragement of university professors when I returned to study, I haven't stopped writing. When I was challenged by Mrs Dunbar, my high school principal, to take up public speaking and participate in essay competitions as a way of having a voice in our community, it was just the beginning (and, much to my surprise, I won). I was motivated even more when I won a scholarship with the Australian Institute of Company Directors for women who aspired to be executives. Today I am invited to write and submit editorials and articles—most recently articles for international business magazines.

While working in the mining industry and then the financial services industry, I was lucky to be surrounded by many talented businessmen and businesswomen, some of whom were Harvard, Oxford, and Cambridge graduates. I observed them at work and noticed that we all have our disciplines and our strengths. The challenge of change processes is to harness the powerful resources that we each have and add to them by sharing our knowledge and skill and by working together to achieve a common goal of making change in business. The greatest challenge in our careers and businesses occurs when we realise that it's time—*now or never*—to make changes in how we are doing business.

Working as part of many large project teams, I have learned that it is essential to be efficient in order to be productive enough to achieve exceptional outcomes. Increasing productivity at work doesn't have to be an overwhelming prospect; it is possible to bring balance to your day and to your employees' actions. You can manage everything you need to do with the right attitude and discipline and some simple techniques.

You can make changes to your business with confidence. Managing change in difficult times requires courage and is a sign of leadership. Making change as an essential part of business growth and development requires an intuitive approach and achieves more than change.

The purpose of this book is to instil a creative, positive, and motivated focus when you make changes in your business. The approach to making changes in *Making Changes Easily* will allow you to gain insight into what you need to consider when making change, how it can be done (whether yours is a small business or a division of a larger organisation), and how to avoid some pitfalls along the way. What you learn will help you make the changes you need to make in your business using the explanations, many techniques, tools, and tips provided to support you.

Each of the chapters is dedicated to a topic related to change and the management of change. There is a chapter dedicated to developing your vision, brainstorming the best of those ideas, setting goals, putting it together, setting out stages of the plans for the changes you wish to make, and using effective communication to improve results. There is also an "ER" section to help you correct your course when things go wrong and put your Change Train[1] back on track with the wheels turning.

The two key parts of making change are to start and to finish. Even if it's just one thing that you wish to change, starting the change is key. Get into a rhythm, and keep moving forward with each change idea, emphasising consistent momentum. Once you have finished one change challenge, move to the next. There will be no limit to making change and achieving it easily.

Once you have started your change process, following the ten steps will help you to finish at least one of your change ideas. Finish what you start, taking small steps

---

[1] The time2manage Change Train Technique®© includes segments of styling the change project development.

each time. Managing daily workloads, business activities, and our private lives can be an overwhelming juggle that results in our being pre-occupied with personal and professional issues. Reading motivating articles and business magazines can prompt us into action, but they take us only part of the way, and sometimes we are left guessing as to what happens next.

Thank you for picking up this book. I hope the ideas and suggestions it contains help you as much as they have helped me in many of the business situations I have been in and in the projects I have been fortunate enough to be part of over the years.

Chapter One, "Know What Change Is," focuses on recognising change and how to go about making it happen for you. Chapter Two, "Develop Your Vision for Your Change Ideas," helps you take your ideas from the dream state and to making it real, which is a big step for some people. Chapter Three, "Brainstorm Change Ideas and Workshop the Best Ideas," takes you and your employees on the first steps of a journey to being creative and selective about the ideas that will become your reality. Chapter Four, "Motivation and Commitment to Change" covers the importance of the energy required to make changes, as any change project is usually undertaken along with normal business activities and will require more resources than usual. Chapter Five, "Change the Way Your Business Thinks—Step by Step," considers how well you know your business, your employees, and your customers. Your business culture and dynamic are critical components of the changes you are proposing to make, and getting your employees on board with the change is a sure way to achieve the best result, while not having them on your side is risky.

Chapter Six, "Principles for Planning Change," provides a few of the basic concepts about planning. I avoided providing too much academic data in this section, as this is a guide to help you start and finish your change ideas, and I didn't want to bog you down in theory. Chapter Seven, "Essential Change Management Practices and Rules," helps you understand the foundation of change through a practical and accessible discussion. Chapter Eight, "Techniques and Tips," uses real-life examples to guide you through the change process and provides ways to start working on your changes. Chapter Nine, "Change and Productivity," explains how to monitor how you make changes in your business without productivity issues' affecting your resources and revenue. While the preceding chapters provide valuable information about how to make changes, Chapter Ten, "Putting It All Together," is a strategy in itself that includes considerations of what changes you yourself are undergoing just by coming up with change ideas. You need your mind on your side, energy, support, and a bundle of other important resources to make this idea a reality. Throughout the chapters are tables, example responses, and explanations to help you work through each change idea you may have.

To achieve success you will need help. Use what you have and then add to it to achieve what you want. You can use six of the best to get you started, thanks to Rudyard Kipling's six serving men: the who, how, when, why, what, and where. Then in Chapter Eight you will dress things up with a little colour using Edward de Bono's "Six Hats" from the book of the same name. The chapter provides his ideas on *parallel thinking*, as they are helpful techniques for recognising the styles of the people on your change team.

Today you took the first of many major steps to plot your course for change: you made the move to read this book, review the guidelines, and take the first practical steps to bring about the change you aspire to achieve. The very fact that you had this vision of change is exciting. Your change story will unfold when you review the basic concepts of change ideas and managing the change process, supported by the questions posed in the guidelines and the template tables.

One of the features of this book is that is provides not only the change concepts and considerations but also a series of sample templates and checklists to help you put your change ideas into action. The templates are simple tools;

if you prefer, you can also use higher-level IT project management software to duplicate the concepts. Use whatever tools you feel comfortable using.

The guidelines at the end of each chapter complement the chapter's message and support you on your change journey. The series of questions for each chapter will assist you in contemplating what change you want to make and to make notes in answering those questions.

The learning objectives for making changes easily are to (1) know what change is; (2) develop your vision of your change ideas; (3) brainstorm the change ideas; (4) sustain, your and your employees' motivation for and commitment to the change; (5) prepare a plan and tweak it along the way; (6) know what your business thinks and the effect of your change plans on it; (7) understand the principles and planning that matter; (8) develop effective change management practices and rules; (9) remember techniques, tools, tips, and tactics; (10) understand change and its effect on productivity; (11) know how to put it all together; and (12) develop a "Back-up plan" when something goes wrong.

Not until a person is motivated and has the right attitude toward making change can change occur. It usually takes a significant event for people to change; a crisis or "hitting bottom" may create a shift in a person that motivates him or her to make a change. Motivation is influenced not only within ourselves but also by our human connections, whether family, friends, or our teams at work.

Creating motivation for change usually requires that we confront potential conflicts from time to time. We confront fear of change and a perceived inability to make change. Denial of the need to make changes is yet another component of our personal response to change. With all of this in mind, let's get started. In facilitating seminars and workshops that include solutions tailored to suit the each business I work with, I am always happy to see the participants' enthusiasm and excitement when they start to get traction on the change ideas they are working on.

**It's time** to manage change, so put the jug on, brew that cup of tea or coffee, and sit down and write out answers to the questions in each chapter. This book and its guidelines will prompt you to answer most, if not all of those initial pressing change questions. You can do this. **It's time!**

# CHAPTER 1

# KNOW WHAT CHANGE IS

> You are here… to enable the world to live more amply, with greater vision, with a finer spirit of hope and achievement. You are here to enrich the world. —Woodrow Wilson

When making change, you must consider the *right place, the right time, and the right people*. Understanding the scale of the change you are about to undertake will relieve some of the pressure and frustration later on and ensure that, if it is engineered correctly, you will achieve change successfully. Managing change and the various risks along the way is essential.

The two key parts of making change are to start and to finish. Only when you have finished one change challenge idea should you move to the next one. Following this simple process will give you limitless possibilities in making changes easily in your business.

If you follow a step-by-step your plan, you will achieve your change idea and finish what you start, taking small steps each time. Our daily lives are full of activities, whether at work or at home, so be alert to becoming too preoccupied with personal and professional issues. You may choose to seek out motivating articles and business magazines that will provide possible solutions, but they take us only part of the way, and sometimes we are left guessing as to what is next.

Most of the change that is experienced in any size of business is external to the business. Most businesses *react* to change instead of *driving* it. The economy, consumers, technology, and legislation have profound impacts on why businesses have to make changes. Over the past decade the mining industry has developed technologies to meet the demand to dig out minerals at a faster and more economical rate, increasing the sophistication of not only the computers but the trucks and rigging. Laws and regulations that govern the safety and health of workers in this type of environment multiply as do the laws and regulations governing the financial services industry to protect consumers and their investments.

A smart business leader is always looking at how to sustain, grow, and keep the business moving forward. Interruptions to business momentum, such as mismanagement or failure to meet the market on products and services, are the biggest impediments to these goals.

Clearly, fundamental rules of application govern any visionary change you may have. Working as part of a team in large projects, I noticed that there were just two rules: The first is that you should always go for quality services and products, not cheaper ones. The second is that, to keep the wheels turning, the vision for your business must be supported by a long-term strategy and a talented management team that can sustain change, drive innovation, accept risk, and meet business margins.

Businesses that grow are also subject to the consequences of environmental changes, so someone must recognise that something different is needed or a gap needs to be filled to improve the dynamics of the business. Alternatively, the product that rests in a niche market is important. In either case, the need for the business to grow may be one that the current business approach cannot accommodate or achieve.

The *Macquarie Dictionary* defines the verb "to change" as "to make a difference, alter in condition, appearance."

## Who is affected by change?

People are affected by change in a variety of ways. They want to see that the difference will be, in fact, a difference, that when they have altered something, it will stay altered and make a difference. The effects are dependent on the individual's level of development and experiences in business and on his or her preparedness to make changes.

In *The 100 Absolutely Unbreakable Laws of Business Success,* Brian Tracy,[2] says, "Change is inevitable. Change is not only inevitable it is also unavoidable."

The most important of the changes to be made is the "who," the stakeholders in this change process, the employees who are affected by or who affect the company's actions. Internal and external to your business, stakeholders have an interest in something your company is doing or planning to do. For example, businesses' stakeholders can include staff, customers, and third-party service providers, legislators, regulators, community leaders, investors, customers, consumers, suppliers, and employees, to name a few.

All stakeholders are important, but your and their priorities and focus may change over time based on the issue and factors like influence, knowledge, credibility, and legitimacy in relation to the changes to be made.

Stakeholder engagement occurs when your company initiates open, two-way discussions in order to understand and find solutions to issues of mutual concern. This engagement happens when your company wants to consider the views and involvement of an individual or a group of employees when making and implementing a

---

[2] Tracy, Brian. (2002). *The Laws of Business Success.* San Francisco, California: Berrett-Kochler.

business decision. This is not the same thing as "delivering a message" or convincing a group to agree with you. The simple action of involving your stakeholders in the change in order to include their needs and expectations will establish, improve, and sustain the value of what they can expect from you and your business services. Conducting surveys of your customers as to what they like and don't like about your product and services often is the starting point. The feedback can lead to some significant changes as to what new product or service you deliver going forward.

As consumers we can all relate to Ernst & Young's Global Consumer Banking Survey 2012. The survey was undertaken to determine how to increase loyalty and satisfaction among the company's customers. While overall satisfaction remained high, trust levels remained low globally, and customers were demanding more customised attention, products, and services from their banks.

Stakeholders may also be any group in your business that is charged with planning, managing, monitoring, and executing a project. Whether the change you are proposing is planning for the long term, improved marketing, a change in your sales approach, or developing a position in the marketplace, it is important to involve your stakeholders before and during the process to achieve better overall outcomes.

## How do we change?

Humans being what they are, we are subject to habits. When we acknowledge what we are sensing, what we feel, and then act accordingly, it is because of what we have learned.

If you sense that something is not right in your business, you're probably right, even when what is precisely wrong is not always clear. All you sense is that you need to bring about change in your business. Headlines in the newspapers and interviews in the media outline new and improved products and services every day. If we hear about changes in the industry we work in, the focus of our attention and emotions shifts.

I challenge you to consider what needs to change in your business and whether what you are proposing to change will make a real difference. Consider doing things differently when making change in your business will have a positive outcome.

I learned an important concept from one of my first bosses, who was the general manager of operations. He told me, "Never delegate a task to anyone unless you know how to do it yourself." This advice has held me in good stead in every job I have had since, as well as in every business I have worked with. If you follow this rule, you will fully understand the true value of any change you propose and the tasks, the time, the effort, and the benefits of working with employees who know that you fully understand and support them. Therefore, one of the first important steps is to work on yourself first.

## When should we change?

Change can be planned, or it can be a knee-jerk reaction, depending on the circumstances. When a well-thought-out plan is executed effectively, you will have an outcome that is close to your visions of change. This is the quality that I referred to earlier—one of two rules to remember through the change process. In the case of reactionary change, you are responding to an emergency with a quick response rather than a thorough application. The thought processes for both planned and unplanned change are complex. When a business has to make changes, whether they are financial, product, or service changes, there is an element of fear and uncertainty.

If a change is based on fear, it is likely to be unplanned and less likely to flow efficiently or effectively. You've heard the adage, "If you fail to plan, you plan to fail." Prepared change that is supported by well-designed plans, demonstrates strength, credibility, and foresight. As a business owner, executive, senior manager, or team leader on whom the task of making the change rests, you have to consider the employees who make up the business, but you must also need to make changes within yourself for yourself first. This consideration and approach can fulfil your expectation that others will change around you because they will want to change with you.

## Why should we change?

The purpose of change can be survival, such that one's very existence relies on embracing change. During environmental changes like economic downturns, many businesspeople have had to make some difficult business decisions, including downsizing of personnel or divisions and reviewing products, services, and locations (branches). Such changes may relate to decisions made years earlier, and what you now see is a product of those past choices. In making changes now, we need to decide what is most likely to work this time based on what we have learned from our experiences. As Pearl S. Buck wrote, "Every great mistake has a halfway moment, a split second when it can be recalled and perhaps remedied." It may be necessary to make more changes now, and the fact that you noticed that change was necessary or inevitable shows you are well on your way to achieving your change goals.

Life isn't perfect, and we have all made errors of judgment in our business decisions. It takes a strong person to recognise that something didn't work and to be prepared to admit and fix the error. Even minor changes for your business can improve one component of your business immediately. The results may be subtle or they may be obvious to all who participate, as may be the recognition that the changes were necessary. The line is often blurred by our ownership of an idea. This blurred vision can create conflicts that widen the gap between the current state and the desired state. Holding fast to "this is my idea, and it's my way or the highway" creates conflicts that are usually difficult to overcome.

For example, while I was working at the head office of a mining company whose office lease was ending, I saw the shift in focus from the mine-site issues to where the head office team would operate. This change came at a time of a downturn in the industry and an increase in lease fees. We needed an office to work from but wondered whether we needed the office to overlook the harbor. Mining has always been about image and strategic location and positioning, but spending a lot of money on a new lease would take away from the mine sites' operational funds. Clearly, then, when we make decisions to bring about change, there are many things to consider. In our case, we decided to spend the money only if the placement of our office was critical to the overall delivery of our products and services. Remember that the way you have done things has culminated in what is before you now. Doing things differently will produce different outcomes.

Other examples of change that you may have seen on television in recent years include examples from *Undercover Boss*. Some of the examples I reviewed included the CEO of the 7-Eleven Store chain of stores, who saw waste, failure to promote enthusiastic employees, and so on; the CEO of Domino's Pizza, who identified how to fix it when the delivery to the customer is late, keeping the customers happy; and the CEO of US-based Turf Club, who recognised employees who went beyond the call of duty. Many of the businesses in the series were family-based companies whose CEOs had inherited the business and discovered that they had become too tied up being the CEO of a large corporation. Their journey undercover sent them back to the basics to see where there were opportunities for growth and improvement in their own businesses.

## What should change?

The answer to what should change is up to you and your trusted advisors. The change may be a change to only a simple component of your business, or a series of ideas and concepts may need to be introduced in pursuit of a far greater result. Alternatively, you may need to change products and services, or they may simply need refreshing.

Planning and setting goals within the planning process will help to ensure the best outcome. As a business leader or a leader of change, you must keep track of trends and review how they fit with your ideas and your business strategy for change. If you don't know what has changed in the marketplace, do some research in order to understand what is likely to be happening "out there" and what could make you stumble if you don't act now. Through well-developed plans and the accumulation of necessary resources, you can keep the progress of the project under control. New situations and the requisite focus will allow you to make progress toward your redefined change programme. It is important to remember that, for the best outcome, change should be disciplined and logical, rather than emotional and volatile.

## Where should change take place?

Change can start with you as a business owner. In a small business there may be one to twenty employees involved. In a medium-sized or larger business, change may have to be made one department or team at a time. Although it is rarely just one thing that needs changing, this approach will allow for the resurgence of energy and creativity that keep individuals and teams motivated and on track with the change programme. Applying the guidelines to each of the things you want changed will allow you to make better plans and improve your progress at the same time as you calculate the risks of making changes. The ripple effect of the change programme can be positive and effective for those who are watching the process. This process can inspire those that are involved, and when a team makes the first change and exceeds expectations, it motivates those around them to follow suit.

Therefore, when people follow a successful leader, it enhances the participants' outlook and encourages those who are less likely to make changes easily. Organisational change requires the same amount of energy and a consistent and direct effort as that required to make changes within ourselves. It takes time to adjust to a new way of doing something and to be effective in the new way. This period of adjustment is developed and explained later in the book.

Small businesses are usually the equivalent of one department, but in larger organisations it often takes only one division to change (positively) before others will catch on to the idea and want to follow suit. Usually, in a smaller business, the only person who needs to change is you, and that requires some "tough love" and a lot of commitment. As for managers of larger businesses, change requires an equal commitment from those who came up with the change ideas and those who participate in the change programme.

Repeat after me (and this is the only time you are allowed to swear during your change process): "I do solemnly swear that I am committed to making these changes.

Here is your chance to make a difference in your life and your business. Start making those changes *today*. You have made the first big move, so make this as interesting as you possibly can and have fun doing it.

## Guidelines for defining change

The series of questions outlined in Table 1 will stimulate you into action by ensuring that you will be clear about change. There are also sample comments to prompt change ideas. For example, the first question is "What do you want to change?" Perhaps your answer is: "I want to rearrange the layout of my home office." If so, firstly look around you and if you are sitting at your home office desk or are at work, look at the position of your desk. What do you want to change? Is it all the stuff that's on the desk? Should there be more drawers or storage to hold your files, folders, and pens? What type of organiser do you need for your pens? Will you need a bigger and better filing system for current items, with consideration for growth in the next few years?

Then when viewing your surrounding area more closely. What other pieces of equipment and tools do you need to improve your work area? Is your desk wide enough? Do you need a bigger computer screen or a second computer screen? Do you need a better ergonomic chair or a footrest?

If you are in a large organisation, look around you at those in your area. Are you sitting in a quiet area or a noisy zone? Once you look closely and actually see things that need improving, you will see your divisions and team members differently. Then you will be able to review each division, one at a time, until you have made a review of the whole organisation. Use the list of questions in Table 1 and work through answering them. When you do prepare your list, ensure that you include your stakeholders, employees, customers, and third-party service providers.

| Question | Answer | Reminder notes |
|---|---|---|
| What does change mean to you? | · By rearranging the office space, I will be able to increase productivity.<br>· Space will be used more efficiently, and paper waste will be reduced, along with and other materials that are left around to become usable. | · The activities in the designated area<br>· The people in the designated area<br>· The items that need to be purchased to make the changes |

## Making Changes Easily

| | | |
|---|---|---|
| Why are you making this change now? | • I've noticed a decrease in productivity and comments coming from the workers.<br>• Other staff in the area are being disrupted by all the discussions being undertaken in the area.<br>• The noise has increased as a result of the issues with the equipment. | • Ensure the printing machines are close to the work area.<br>• Ensure that the machine is multi-purpose.<br>• There is a need for extra tables for collating booklets, etc.<br>• There is a need for cupboards for all the different types of paper, covers, plastics, and binding rings. |
| Who will be affected by the change you are going to make? (List your stakeholders and the pros and cons of the changes.) | • All employees in the office space. | • Place the photocopiers, printings, binding machines, and stationary in a central area. |
| How are you going to make these changes? (Anticipate what your stakeholders will need to know about.) | • Check your equipment budget.<br>• Seek suppliers to provide equipment that will meet all of your needs now and going forward. | • Look at a significant upgrade to equipment and its capabilities. |

| | | |
|---|---|---|
| | · Seek suppliers who are prepared to train your employees once their products are installed.<br>· Seek suppliers who are close to your office who will be available if their products need servicing. | · Plan the training sessions on the day the equipment is installed to reduce delays in productivity.<br>· Address any particular needs to be met (projects, divisional requirements, printing of monthly reports, deadlines, etc.). |
| Where will this change take place? | · If you are only one office, ensure that you seek suppliers who understand your workloads and the needs of your outputs for new products and equipment. It may be feasible to have two smaller versions of a needed piece of equipment, rather than one larger, so you have a back-up if one should break down. | · Double-check requirements for servicing and supplies.<br>· Acquire security access codes for specific tasks and cost allocations. |

| When will this change take place? | • Check the teams' schedules. If the problem is apparent, give the teams notice of the change and the approximate turnaround time and training time on any new moves to rearranging the office and possibly any new equipment you are proposing to introduce to increase productivity. | • Put up the new layout/design around the office.<br>• Arrange for basic instructions to be laminated and placed in front of any new equipment. |
|---|---|---|

Table 1: Making the Decision for Change

Following the process outlined in Table 1 will ensure that you (a) understand the nature of the change for you, (b) understand your own willingness and ability to change at this time, (c) identify what you want to change and why, and (d) develop a framework that will lead your change ideas effectively.

Another example is the configuration of the office space, whether this is your home office, or a small to medium-sized business office. There are usually phones ringing, people talking, and people walking around the office, so consideration for the needs of each team must be part of the configuration. For example, it is counterproductive to place the finance team next to a sales team, as the finance team requires a quieter environment than a sales area, with phones constantly ringing and telephone discussions being held. Another example if you are looking to streamline your office is to centralise all meeting rooms so they are away from the work area. The meeting rooms can be of various sizes to ensure that the smallest and the largest groups of people are served.

Steps that you can complete and expand on as you progress through the change process for each idea include (1) preparing plans and procedures for how you will make change happen for your business, (2) determining whom do you need to include in these plans and procedures, (3) preparing and communicating the plan behind the change, (4) identifying what the outcome should be for your business, (5) ensuring communications and presentations are clear when you deliver the message, (6) discussing the changes with those involved to ensure that they understand them fully, (7) ensuring acceptance of the change among all stakeholders, (8) following up on progress made with those involved.

## Chapter Summary

Main point 1: What do you want to change? Are you clear on what that is?

Main point 2: What do you need to do to make it happen?

Main point 3: What needs to be considered in the planning this change to achieve the best outcome?

Now that we've discussed what change is, let's move on to your ideas and developing your vision of what changes you'd like to make in your business.

## CHAPTER 2

# DEVELOP YOUR VISION OF YOUR CHANGE IDEAS

> Visions are powerful mental images of what we want to create in the future. They reflect what we care about most, and are harmonious with our values and sense of purpose… The tension we feel from comparing our mental image of a desired future with today's reality is what fuels a vision. — Edward de Bono, education and learning consultant

So you have this vision. You have an idea or two or three or more. They're creative ideas, and you want something changed as soon as possible. Your vision needs to be simple, strategic, and driven correctly and efficiently to achieve the best sustainable change outcome. Know what it is that you want to change. Name it, describe it, and even draw a picture of it. You need to know exactly what it is.

What do you feel when you think of this change idea? How motivated are you about it? Are you beginning to feel uncomfortable? Are you excited? Are you *really* excited? Do you feel that you just can't wait? With this kind of strong feeling you'll certainly move toward your goal quickly. Your mind may be racing with questions, and you may be in a sort of state of wonder about it all: *I wonder whether it would work if I did this or that? I wonder whether I will make money out of this? I wonder what will happen if it doesn't work?* and so on. You will be asking yourself other questions too, such as *Where do I start?* It's always good to start at the beginning.

One way to ignite your business is to know your business. To effectively describe what is it about your business that would interest people, you need to know your audience.

There must have been something compelling to prompt you to think about this change idea or concept, that has made you want to act on the change idea straight away and see it through. Even if you have only one idea, it may take all of the principles, processes, practices, planning, techniques, rules of change, hard work, sweat, tears, and effort you can muster to achieve it.

When embarking on a journey of any type, it is always important to be prepared and to be in the right frame of mind. As part of the preparation for this journey of change, find a quiet location and be still for a time. Be in the moment so you can centre yourself when you are experiencing difficulties in the change project. Before you make a list of ideas of things you want to change or what could go wrong with your situation, consider acknowledging first what is good about the situation you are in and how well you cope under pressure. There are benefits in learning to relax and meditate. Learning to achieve a balance in your physical, mental, emotional, and spiritual energies will help your body revitalise.

If you don't know how to be still and remain calm in a crisis, it would be a good idea to learn this technique. If you are rushing and tired, then you may not be able to concentrate sufficiently to apply yourself to the task or last the distance to bring about change successfully.

Focus on the positives of the situation. Once you have achieved clarity, prepare the list of what you want to change to enhance what you have—the aspects of your business to be improved. It may be an efficiency issue, one of cost effectiveness, or equipment upgrades. If you need a printer, consider that may not only reduce your printing and paper costs but also excite your employees, be less likely to break down during high production and peak times, deliver clearer copies or a more robust colour scheme, and result in less frustration for all users.

If your computer or telephone system needs an upgrade to improve your communications with your customers, seek suppliers who guarantee their products. Bragging rights in relation to the latest technology is usually high on employees' lists of conversational topics when they interact with people outside the office.

The next step is to take the best ideas from your list and act on them. You don't have to do this alone or in isolation. Always consider asking for help from a trusty advisor or, if your idea involves technology with which you're not familiar, a professional.

On a piece of paper write down the heading "My Vision of Change Is...," and then complete the statement. Asking yourself the right questions and then asking the same questions of other people may give you a bigger, better, different picture of change. The other people you consult may include the change leader you have nominated if you aren't planning on being in charge of the change yourself. When you have buy-in to these change ideas at a high level, the success rate is higher.

## What is your vision for this change?

Sun Tzu's philosophy for vision is simple: "Use the normal force to engage; use the extraordinary to win."[3] So how extraordinary are you going to be when you build this vision of change?

| Question | My Vision for change |
| --- | --- |
| What is my vision of change? | My vision of change is… |
| Why do I want to make this change? | I want to make this change because… |

---

[3] Michaelson, Gerald. *Sun Tzu for Success.* Avon, MA: Adams Media, 2003.

| | |
|---|---|
| How will the change be made? | I will make this change by brainstorming with the managers first and then the individual teams. |
| When will I make this change? | I will make this change… Date of the commencement of change: Date of the outcome of change: |
| Where will the change be made? | I will make the change in marketing and customer services. |
| Who will make the change? | I will arrange for a change manager to oversee the changes I want to make. |

Table 2: The Change Vision Statement

Whom you put in charge of change is as important as the outcome of the change you are proposing. You need to see the outcome clearly in your mind at all times. What is it that you see right now? Hold that thought. First, you make the plan, then you set timeframes, and finally you set progress stages. Then you work through the stages in sequence. (The Appendix has blank samples of these forms for you.)

- The Plan: write down your plan, keep good notes, and then work through the process. (Of course, "write" could refer to making notes or tasks on your mobile phone, iPad, tablet, or project management software.)
- Timeframes: Prepare a timetable with a number of stages.[4]

---

[4] The guidelines contain a series of templates to assist you.

- Progress Stages: When you start to roll out the plan, start with one step, finish it and then move on to the next step of the plan.

## How do you put your vision into action?

If you have not been good at writing plans, then it is important to get good at it now! If you see yourself only as the "vision" person, then work with someone who is skilled in the planning process. Writing down as many ideas as you can think of will be beneficial in the long term to ensure that your change process has a firm foundation. These plans are vital to achieving the best outcome. Start with the overview and then develop the plan by putting the ideas and activities into stages of development and delivery, including holding a meeting with your change team. The agenda template provided will ensure you stay on point.

**Tips:**

- Appoint a change champion or change leader.
- Consider using an outsider to facilitate and help move things forward.
- Ensure regular communication with the team.
- Keep employees motivated and handle resistance.
- Ensure that there are links among your vision, your values, and the change you are proposing.

## When do you put your vision into action?

You can put your vision into action once you have done your due diligence—the homework, the research, the review of available resources, the goals that form part of the action plan and the ultimately the overall project plan. Each business can have its own specialised type of due diligence. For example, mining due diligence includes surveying and project engineering for all the equipment and the labour requirements for the duration of the operations. In financial services, due diligence includes risk analysis and underwriters for each type of product.

Having employees with the right skill sets to achieve the outcome you are working toward is just one of the top priorities. What do your customers want? If you don't know, ask. SurveyMonkey is a handy online product that is easy to use and a good place to start asking some simple questions of your customers and employees. As part of your due diligence establish what the competition is doing. You may have a similar idea, but new packaging or delivery of the product or service may be the key to customers deciding to use your product instead.

Doing your homework and preparing good notes increases your chances of success, so prepare clearly defined plans for your change idea(s) to allow your strategy to unfold and achieve the best outcomes.

## How excited are you now?

Ascertain whether your team members or participants share your passion for the change. This shared experience of excitement sustains motivation for the project overall.

## Where do you put your vision into action?

Where you put your vision into action depends on how you undertake your meetings. A semi-formal setting is ideal. Take the meeting outside of the office initially—in another venue if possible, such as at a conference centre. The arrangements that you make for the initial change meeting are important to the overall acceptance of your vision of change. Developing a first impression of what is about to occur and the invitation to a "meeting of the minds" requires a lot of thought. Planning is important.

Ensure that you have a meeting agenda and sufficient time for discussions to be completed. (Not all topics need to be debated intensely or even need to form part of the discussion.) Use your list of ideas to allow participants to understand your "big picture." They need to understand what you are proposing to change.

Once you have shared your ideas, they will know what you expect them to deal with. This opportunity allows them to digest the process and then create the win-win scenario you are looking for. A good start is to know what they want. You can use surveys to gather information about your ideas and what your employees would like to see in the change process. Then it is up to you to use the information you receive to motivate your employees to be part of the change process.

Invite participation to determine what they want and what they need. For example, if you are considering installing top-of-the-line coffee/tea-making equipment, your employees won't have to leave the office as often to go to a coffee shop, saving time and money for the business. But is this what they want? Is there an advantage to their taking a break to go to the coffee shop that you haven't considered?

## Why are you putting your vision into action in this way?

It has to be as much about them, as it is about you. Your employees need confidence in you and to be able to trust that you will bring them through to the conclusion of your change plan. There will be times when you need the speed and precision of a rally driver to bring about the change. When the change must be swift, ensure that they understand that time counts. When the change requires greater involvement, participation, and consideration, then take it down a notch, prepare the step-out plan, allow them to keep up, and ensure you help them do the catch-up they must do to make these changes while also doing their usual activities.

Generally, employees don't like being unable to finish their tasks each day, and the work can build up when there is change that requires extra work. As a result, some things can be missed or forgotten. Put yourself in their shoes: Some employees may not "get it" until they are close to the end result, as their image of what you want changed may not be quite the same as yours. You are challenging them to step out of their comfort zones. What may appear to be resisting change may simply be an inability to understand the change as well as you do.

> Instructional intelligence studies have provided many insights into work behaviours based on the different generations. What is important to one is not as important to the other generation.[5]

Knowing your employees and your other stakeholders is essential. One way to bolster your knowledge bank in this area is to do surveys on features of the change project. Your employees, your customers, and your service providers will appreciate that their ideas have

---

[5] Gregory, Gayle H., and Carolyn Chapman. (2007). *Differentiated Instructional Intelligence: One Size Doesn't Fit All*. Thousand Oaks, California, Corwin Press.

been considered and incorporated into your change process. They will know that you listened.

## Who will put your vision into action?

Who puts your vision into action depends on what is going to change. You may need to consider using a change leader, to consider the resources you may or may not have available, and your employees' skill sets. Where resources allow, choose a capable and compatible change leader who will support the changes, challenge your stakeholders, and achieve your desired results.

If resources don't allow you to hire a dedicated change leader, then you may want to choose one from your existing team. The person will need to be well liked, respected, and experienced in undertaking this type of project.

> It is true that a few people are born to be successful. They possess some special talent that makes it easy to succeed [like]the gifted musician, the natural athlete… [However,] the vast majority of successful people were not handed their success on a silver platter."[6]

---

[6] Trump, Donald, and Bill Zanker. (2007). *Think Big and Kick Ass in Business and Life*. New York: Collins.

You can achieve anything if you make the right choice and plan well.

## Envision the outcome

Show me a person who is enthusiastic, and I guarantee that he or she knows that enthusiasm catches on quickly, that it beats anyone with profound knowledge, and that enthusiasm generates high energy among the team. Persevere and you will accomplish great things. Don't ask someone to do something that you are not prepared to do or won't do yourself. If you have to, it may only be a temporary fix, and doesn't have long-term benefits for you or your employees.

One question you must answer concerns whether what you are proposing will cause such conflict that it is more trouble than it's worth. In that case, will you still go ahead with it? People aren't gullible. Trying to get employees to do something that you want without due process and consideration can be a mistake, so don't lull yourself into a false sense of security that employees will do as they are told and not react. When their instincts tell them that something is not quite right, especially if they know from their own personal or professional experience that there's an easier or better way to achieve this change idea, resistance will result. Resistance will also occur if they become overloaded with tasks that are part of the change plan while trying to maintain the "business as usual" in their daily work.

Alice in Alice in Wonderland asked the Cheshire Cat, "Would you tell me, please, which way I ought to go from here?" The Cheshire Cat replied, "That depends a good deal on where you want to get to." Knowing where you want to be at the end of the change project is central to its success, so plan your daily activities in advance and move in a straight line. When you stay focused in this way, you conserve your energy and finish your activities faster. When you allow distractions to interrupt you, you lose time and energy, which impacts all types of resources.

Consideration, communication, checks, balances, and strong leadership and support help to ensure a good outcome. Embrace the target, start with creating a win-win situation, work with the end in mind, and keep up the momentum throughout the change process. Keep the image of the desired outcome well entrenched in your mind and in the minds of your employees. It takes more than a completed series of tasks to arrive at the change you want to bring about.

Write down the steps you are going to take to make change, including taking small breaks to allow you to step back and see the progress being made. Some employees can plan ahead and manage their workloads and personal interests so they are excited about everything, but for

## Making Changes Easily

many people, change represents work and no holidays until it's done. That can be a depressing thought that leaves us feeling demotivated and frustrated.

The thought that you have to achieve your normal workload along with all this other *stuff* to do can be very distracting and distressing. It can result in being inefficient at work while you slowly pick up the pace. To help you and your employees feel excited and in control of their work-life plans, consider encouraging your employees to think about what they want to do that year in terms of holidays, exercise, hobbies, and other activities that they enjoy. If you allow them to be involved in the plan for their days and weeks in advance according to their own schedule, they are more likely to feel better about going to work in the first place.

And given how much time is spent at work, it's important to feel happy while we are there. I suggest that people take several steps to establish a good balance between work and their private life:

- Before you set any business appointments on your weekly calendar, set appointments for yourself, including exercise, time out for yourself, for family, and for friends.
- Look at your annual calendar and decide when you'd like to take holidays: make a definite plan and book in dates now for your next break.

- Plan mini-escapes every month: They do not need to be expensive; they can be a night away with your partner or a few hours at the beach reading a book, but be sure you lock it in and do it.

Other ideas include providing assistance for the teams you ask to work on the project while doing their current workload. You may also need to rethink the key performance indicators on current business activities during the expansion project. Follow a set pattern to sustain energy levels and momentum. The aim is not to run out of vital energy and miss out on achieving the change project.

## Who will see what you see?

Ensuring that others see what you see is achieved by effective communication, demonstration, and clarity applied to what it is that you want changed and who you want to follow you in making it happen. Ask your employees and your stakeholders what they are going to do and how they can contribute to the outcome.

People always like to do things they enjoy doing, are good at, and are comfortable doing. It's all about enthusiasm and energy; when they know what the outcome is going to be, their enthusiasm brings them joy and gratification with the outcome. Keep them involved in the process. You may be surprised when you discuss your plans with them and receive feedback like "It's about time" or "I was wondering when we could do something like this." This shows that they like the idea, are receptive to some of the change plans, and will work with you on it. They must trust you and have confidence that you will employ the right talent and skills to allow them all to work together as a team to achieve the outcome. Once you have it, keep the momentum; if things drag on or come to a halt, resuming momentum may not be easy to achieve. Keep moving with the flow of the project activities, and be vigilant.

You can maximise the outcome of your day by following these four simple steps:

- At the end of your day, make a list of what you need to do and amend your to-do list.
- Allow 10 minutes to put the list together: Place the list in the most visible location in your office so when you return in the morning it's all in the one spot and you are ready to go.
- Handle things once: When you start a task, ensure that you complete it. Finish one task before you move to the next one.
- Set aside specific times for reading, making phone calls, and speaking with your team. Informative and meaningful communication is far more

effective than several piecemeal comments. Meetings are for achieving solutions, not for hours of discussion and explanations because people haven't kept up with reading their memos.

## What resources do you need to put into the vision?

The resources for realising your vision come back to money most of the time. How much do you need to spend? Sometimes you need to spend money to make money, but be sensible about your approach if your resources are limited. Know how much money it is likely to take to achieve your vision. Be informed, calculate it, and be realistic. All of the enthusiasm and excitement will fall away if you are constantly thinking of the effect of the strain and drain on your finances.

Your change idea may require a staged approach or taking the plunge all at once for the plan to be as effective as it can be. Always expect the unexpected. Always plan for extra expenses in any project. You may need more employees (either temporarily or permanently), extra training, or increases in pricing from the time you start the project to when you finish it. Anticipate that not all features of your change plan will come to fruition. One feature may become a work in progress for the next stage if resources are not available to complete it at the time.

## How will you arrive at the outcome?

Mapping is an effective method for planning your project. The MAP[7] (mastery, autonomy and purpose) approach is discussed in Daniel Pink's book, *Drive*, and there are some videos on YouTube to that describe it. The MAP approach relates primarily to people's motivation, as motivation tends to increase and decrease during the course of a change project. The MAP concept is based on behavioural science research that explains that what motivates people in the workplace more than money is a sense of autonomy, mastery, and purpose. Assuming people are earning an adequate amount of money, their performance increases dramatically when these three elements are present. If you are not interested in such a technical plan or if your project is only a small one, then keep to a basic template and use a simple approach. If you need more information, do some research on how some successful business leaders, such as Guy Kawasaki and Donald Trump, have undertaken change.

## When do you see the vision becoming a reality?

An effective plan that has stages or phases that make sense to all of those involved will keep the ball rolling and sustain the momentum you need to see your vision to fruition. Therefore, when you invite your employees to

---

[7] Kawasaki, Guy. (2007). *Enchantment*. London, England: Penguin.

be part of the change project, seek their ideas about how the plan should unfold. You may be pleasantly surprised at the wealth of talent at your fingertips. If you aren't fully appraised about your employees and their talent base, familiarise yourself about their skills and qualifications.

## What are the stages of change for you?

Where are those notes you made? Where are the checklists and progress reports that you developed? Have you revisited and modified the business plan for this change project? What is the status of each item on those lists? You may need to delegate tasks and responsibilities to make it happen. Don't forget to seek buy-in for your change vision. Apply progressive incentives, and let your stakeholders know what is happening and how it will benefit them. Explain the positives of the improvements and the rewards.

## Who will be responsible for the stages of change?

If you are not the change leader, ensure that he or she has strong project skills, team skills, and communication skills and be well-liked by the participants. The change leader will be responsible for breaking up the change plan into small, manageable pieces and for deciding who will be responsible for each stage. When you lead by example, you will give the participants an idea of what you require of them. The change you are proposing, when broken into small manageable pieces throughout all facets of the project, will allow for clarity.

Keep Rudyard Kipling's "six serving men" working for you. They will help you arrive at your desired outcome by asking *who, how, what, when, where,* and *why*. Answering these questions will help you deliver all stages of the change process.

Even when you are undertaking only basic changes, you still need an introductory phase followed by the main change component and the round-up of all that encompasses the change. For larger projects you will need a further series of stages or phases to ensure that all tasks are achieved. Therefore, decide who will be responsible for stage 1, stage 2, stage 3, and so on.

The change leader may need to change between the stages or phases of your change program if expertise requirements change, but ensure there is traction and continuity in the transition. Each stage has its own core competencies, applications, direction, and momentum.

## Your change checklist

A simple format for a change checklist was provided in Chapter One, and now you need to expand on those questions.

Whether you are planning a simple personal change or a plan for a big change in your business, determine what you want to change. Consider what prompted this desire to change. Was it something you felt from within, something you read or saw on television, or something another business has undertaken that has made it more productive than ever? Are you being realistic in what you want to change? Why do you want the change? How do you want to change? Whom do you want to change? When do you want the change? (Be realistic!) Where will you end up? Answer these questions honestly, writing down as many answers under each question as you can muster to help you begin to develop your change plan.

Know what you are dealing with. If you are making a change for your business, take time to make your own changes first to test the traction of those ideas. Do you know what to expect? It's important to know the terrain, as things (and employees) may not always be what they appear. Therefore, choose your project team members carefully. My father shared a few pieces of advice with me over the years that he learned in business, including the observation that "Cheetahs don't change their spots. Cheetahs look different when they are in different terrain, but they are still cheetahs." If you are experiencing discomfort with a person, don't ignore your instincts.

Sometimes we don't see things as we should because we are too busy working, we assume that what we are seeing is not a cheetah, and we get a surprise when they show their true colours by demonstrating that they are not as proactive or prepared to participate in the project as you first thought. In other words, don't have a false sense of security that you know what you are up against. Prepare, prepare, prepare. Like a good craftsman, "measure twice, cut once."

## **Changing why we do what we do**

Three things to consider when making changes are our thinking, our actions, and our outcomes. Once you have realised that you need to make a change and acquired a vision of change, you want a successful outcome. You are where you are in your business because of the decisions you made in your previous strategic plan. Now you are back at step one in wanting to make further changes, so maybe it's time for a different approach.

Is your mind on your side? Are all the minds of your team members going to be working together as one on this project? Do you have a vision statement and a mission statement for your business? Everyone must be on board with the changes to be made and willing to lend their talent to see it through.

Evaluate your actions during the course of the project. Do they show a positive and motivating leader promoting change? Not everyone is meant to lead, so before you start, consider whether you need someone independent and less attached emotionally to the vision in the role of change leader.

Are the outcomes you envision for this change process beneficial to all stakeholders? Do the research to make sure you can answer this question.

If your employees don't understand your expectations are, ask yourself why they don't. You or the change leader (or both) must clarify your expectations for all participants. There is no room for subtlety; spell it out. Provide details on everything from the idea to the phases, the timing, the impacts, and the cost of the project. Ensure that your resources can address the unexpected, examine what is driving the change project, and analyse the tasks involved.

## Vision guidelines for your business

Now you can extend the vision template you started in the first chapter. Define your vision of change; write it down and date it. This is your vision, your idea of change, the idea that will shape the new and improved business you want. The more information and detail in the idea, the more you can share with those you invite on this vision mission.

Be sure to answer the following questions:

(1) *What* is your vision of change? Some examples are the layout of the office, the culture, the bottom line, introducing new technologies, and updating your client listing. Expand on these ideas.
(2) *Why* do you want to change? List reasons for each of the changes you have identified.
(3) By *when* do you propose to achieve the change? Be realistic, and factored in your schedule. Use project management software or even a simple Word document. Don't complicate things unnecessarily
(4) *How* do you want to make the change? List each item. For example, if you want to change the layout of the office, draw up plans on paper, and consider the space, lighting, what can be reused, what needs to be replaced, and so on.
(5) *When* do you want to the change to take place? For example, the layout of the office may require that furniture be moved, so you may need to do this on a weekend so the daily work flow is not disrupted. The time of year may also be a factor, so be aware of priorities in each of your divisions. For example, don't ask your finance department to make substantial changes at the end of a quarter or at the end of a financial year or the marketing team to

make changes when they are launching a new product. Consider scheduled annual leave as well, as you want everyone to be engaged in what you are proposing to do.

**In answering the five preceding questions, be aware that there are five common errors that may occur when making changes:**

- Underestimating the effect of your vision
- Ineffectual communication of your vision
- Failing to create a win-win in the early stages of the change process
- Failing to embed those changes in the business culture quickly
- Failing to create synergies amongst participants

## The ten most common changes needed in business today

Working with dozens of businesses over the past decades, I've found that businesses that are undergoing change projects often benefit from changing certain core concepts in how they do business:

- inner self-talk (from "I can't do this" or "This can't change" to "I can do this" or "this can change")
- priorities (Knowing what your priorities are in the change process will assist you in adjusting

the timeframes and allow you and your team to prioritise the changes you want to make.)
- motivation (generating the right amount of energy and enthusiasm to keep your team going when the going gets tough)
- habits (If you are not strong on setting and achieving goals, you may need to work with people who can guide you through the change process. If you don't set goals and the timeframes to achieve those goals, then it is important to start now or seek support from someone who is good at organising.)
- friends (Supportive friends outweigh negative ones.)
- commitments (the leader's roles and responsibilities)
- how tasks are undertaken (Are you looking at ways to increase productivity in your business?)
- methodologies (Are you focused on being efficient and achieving productive outcomes?)
- passion (focusing on what you love, feel excited about, and are fired up about)
- how money is spent (focusing on achieving results without spending heaps of money)

Leaders in particular must analyse themselves and their strengths and weaknesses when anticipating a change process. Ask yourself:

- How effective are you as a manager? What qualities do you need to have in your current situation? Do you need to select someone from

your office who has some of the skills required choose an independent change project leader?
- How prepared are you to change so you can lead by example and sustain the focus throughout the whole project?
- What might go wrong, and do you have what it takes to fix it?
- What positive things can you say about yourself? Write a list of fifty positive and empowering statements about yourself starting with "I am..." or "I am capable of..."—that will make a difference in how you see yourself in the change process. For example:
- I am capable of being an effective leader for this change process.
- I am capable of finishing this change process on time and on (or under) budget.
- I can make the right choices when it comes to my project team and finish the race.
- I will do this, and we will bring about change for the business.

## What is your personal vision and mission statement for the change project?

Your personal vision statement may read something like this: I share my vision of change with the people in my business. I am confident that, as a team, we can

## Making Changes Easily

achieve great change for the business and its products and services. I will ensure that we have the right skills and talent working on this project and for maintaining the business' ongoing functions for the duration the change. I lead this team to finish the project on time and on budget. I will present and maintain a positive and motivated outlook and environment so my employees can achieve the best outcome for the business and its stakeholders.

You have started on the journey of change by describing your vision and are ready to develop your vision of change through brainstorming and workshopping.

> My mind withdrew its thoughts from experience, extracting itself from the contradictory throng of images, that it might find out what that light was wherein it was bathed… And thus, with the flash of one hurried glance, it attained to the vision of That Which Is. —Saint Augustine

# CHAPTER 3

# BRAINSTORM CHANGE IDEAS AND WORKSHOP THE BEST IDEAS

You can develop change ideas by yourself or with the help of others. This chapter focuses on working with others to brainstorm and workshop change ideas.

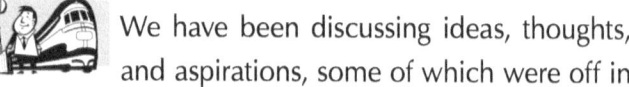 We have been discussing ideas, thoughts, and aspirations, some of which were off in the distance. Now we are embarking on a journey to clarify and solidify these ideas through brainstorming and workshopping.

## Brainstorming

Brainstorming is the downloading of every piece of information about the idea(s) you and your team have for the change project. In a brainstorming session, there can be no analysis of the ideas put forward and no testing or commenting on the idea(s), whether they are good, bad, or ugly. The purpose of a brainstorming session is to do a "brain dump," so every possibility and every bit of information is recorded. Stopping to evaluate what's offered curtails the process.

## Making Changes Easily

Whether yours is a small, medium-sized, or large business, a brainstorming group can be made up of you and a few trusted advisors, such as close business associates, or representatives of stakeholder groups.

Brainstorming with your quorum on your vision of change:

- increases the detail of your ideas and clarifies the involvement and level of engagement required from all participants in the project.
- adds to the detail that your plan requires.
- provides measures required for the ideas.
- gives you a sense of the activities and action items required.
- helps to ensure commitment from the stakeholders.
- encourages all levels of the business to participate and be involved in the change.
- assists you in overcoming any insecurities you may have.
- helps you make the change itself.
- assists you in dealing with the disturbance change creates.
- helps you conquer your fear of failing.

Employees' resist change when it is imposed on them without consultation, consideration, and communication. In your brainstorming session, be ready to write all ideas, notes, comments, and suggestions on a whiteboard or large sheets of chart paper, and keep them to review later. These will form part of the workshopping phase.

If you have a business partner, as is the norm in small businesses, have a few independent third parties to bounce your ideas off. Remember that the essential component is putting down all the ideas of all the participants without comment or criticism. For brainstorming to be effective, it needs to consist of downloading data only. Take care when you share information during these forums that you respect the contribution of participants and resist making negative comments on any ideas put forward. Ensure all participants demonstrate respect when they share any type of information at such events.

Customers' opinions are valuable in brainstorming sessions, so if you haven't asked your customers by way of a survey or you haven't heard what they are saying about you, then maybe it's time you did. Something as simple as the complaints received from people using the elevators in the Trump Towers in Manhattan led to a change. Users perceived that the elevators were slower in the Trump Towers building than were elevators in other buildings in that area. The property maintenance team investigated these complaints but found no significant difference in the elevators' speed. During a brainstorming session held to find a solution to the customers' misperceptions, an interior designer mentioned that the elevators in the Trump Towers had wooden walls, rather than the mirrors some of the other buildings' elevators had. It turned out that the mirrors increased the users' perception of speed and replacing the wooden walls with mirrors reduced complaints about the speed of the Trump Towers' elevators.

Here is one expert's take on how brainstorming should be done. In *Ready, Fire, Aim*, Michael Masterson suggested a formula for creative brainstorming:[8]

First, Masterson suggests gathering at least three people for a brainstorming session. However, he explains that Malcolm Gladwell's book, *The Tipping Point*, suggested eight in order to gather a longer list of ideas to workshop later. This approach may work in large organisations, but it's better for small businesses to keep it simple in the beginning, and start with at least three people for your brainstorming session.

Second, put a time limit on the brainstorming session—an hour or even half an hour—to gather the participants' ideas. If you go for an hour, the second half hour will be time for the participants to work through and establish plans for each idea.

Third, keep standards high in this first session. Focus on the vision, and don't allow distractions or tangents or

---

[8] Masterson, Michael. (2008). *Ready, Fire, Aim.*: Chichester Great Britain John Wiley and Sons.

make the mistake of commenting on the ideas you are reviewing.

Fourth, all the ideas provided by each person are equal, so there should be no comments for or against any of the ideas during brainstorming.

Finally, form a culture where you challenge your people to be innovative and be as creative as possible. In the brainstorming session if you allow participants to download their thoughts and ideas without criticism then you will have a greater pool of ideas to work on in the workshopping session.

While the brainstorming for The Trump Towers issue addressed only one problem, you may need a more developed process for your change process. The method you use depends on the size and scope of your particular change project.

**Another Brainstorming Tip:** If you are not going to brainstorm with your people, then simply write down fifty things you want to see changed in your business. I know fifty seems like quite a few, but doing a "brain dump" is what will reveal the gem amid the rubble.

The ideas put forward in your brainstorming session may also include some personal changes that may also relate and interrelate with other ideas put forward for the business. If each participant writes down a list of ideas and the lists are collated at the end of the brainstorming session, you may be surprised to find that not only are there many ideas, many of the ideas are also similar. Once you collate the full list of ideas, review them for what they have in common. Then pick the top five ideas and consider how important they are in relation to your desire for change right now?

At the end of the brainstorming session, select the best ideas and/or the ones that have the most in common, as selecting ideas with a common thread is a good place to start. Keep improving on your best ideas. You can come back to the other ideas at another time and work on them in another phase of the change process.

## Workshopping

After you have selected the best ideas from your brainstorming session, you can start the next process, workshopping. Here again, ideas are not right or wrong. This is where things are explained in detail, including:

- understanding the change idea itself
- the approach you are considering to make this change
- the policies and processes that will be used to put the change in motion

- the methods you are proposing to use
- the systems to be used

In the workshop process, the leader must:

- emphasise that the ultimate responsibility for change will rest with you; and
- interpret, communicate effectively, and enable (rather than impose or instruct) change

## To start the change process

Now that you've picked the top five or ten ideas, it is time to review them. After a break, reconvene your workshop with your "innovative change advisors" to refine your top ideas.

The focus of this workshop session is to determine how to develop your top ideas. You will need all of your best communication skills and techniques you can muster, with listening being the one you use most. For the smaller business owner, an independent third party who facilitates the session can help keep it from being affected by comments that are too personal or to which you may be too attached. Separating yourself from the ideas will improve the outcome of the workshopping session.

Remember that there are still no wrong or right ideas at this point, although one may need to come before the other. Again, simply contribute as much information and knowledge for each idea to make this work effectively for you.

> **A friendly reminder:** No opinions or criticisms are allowed in workshop sessions. It is simply the next step in the development of this creative collection of ideas from all participants. Avoid doing a head count to see if an idea is liked or disliked or keeping track of who said what and keeping score. Doing any of these things taints the ideas before you even start this process. Good questions include "What can you do to ensure that this idea or concept is successful?" and "How can we do this and get the best result possible?"

Don't allow "FEAR" (Fantasized Experience Appearing Real) to visit this meeting. Have only worthy contributors in your meetings. Stay positive about your vision and sustain the passion. Overcome your fear of failure if one of your ideas isn't selected for additional consideration, as the participants may just not be ready for it yet. While a bit of anxiety can be effective in some circumstances, it can be a major obstacle to the success of your change challenge. Brian Tracy, a professional speaker and author, suggests that you "first affirm to yourself with energy and conviction, "I can do it!"[9] Something so simple can help you overcome feelings of fear and desperation that you can't make these changes happen for your business or team.

Humans are unpredictable creatures. Left to their own devices, they have a tendency to do whatever benefits them, which may not be in your favour. You don't have to control everything, but choosing your team may be more than strategic initially. Many great battles in history have been won by using some of the simplest concepts. However, making the fewest mistakes helps.

Every great mistake has a halfway moment, a split second when it can be recalled and perhaps remedied. —Pearl S. Buck

This quote from Pearl S Buck is one I have relied on when making changes in my business activities. Your plans need to be fluid so you can tweak the plan and process as you go. It's okay if you make a mistake. It's better to start somewhere and do something, make a mistake, and remedy it than to do nothing and never know how far you could have progressed if you had tried. We are all experts in hindsight.

---

[9] Tracy, Brian. (1993). *Maximum Achievement*. New York, First Fireside Edition.

## Making Changes Easily

However, as Sun Tzu pointed out, "By taking into account the unfavourable factors, he may avoid possible disasters."[10] Always anticipate and include the negatives in your plan and provide solutions for them. That means preparing for the unexpected.

Knowing with whom you are dealing can help clarify where you stand when it comes to your family, friends, social group, and role in your organisation. Relationships are not only important, "Relationships are all there is."[11]

You are unique, so know who you are and where you fit in. If you are the CEO, the general manager, the operations or project manager, or a team leader, those around you will observe your behaviour and confidence in the change process throughout the entire process. You are constantly judged by what you say and what you do, so your engagement with others in the activities associated with the roll-out of the change process will make a difference. Clearly define your position when delivering your message of change to your employees.

---

[10] Michaelson, Gerard, and Stephen Michaelson. (2003). *Sun Tzu for Success*. Avon, MA: Adams Media.

[11] Michaelson, Gerard, and Stephen Michaelson. (2003). *Sun Tzu for Success*. Avon, MA: Adams Media (with reference to Wheatley and Kellner-Rogers' *A Simpler Way*).

In summary, brainstorming with your team on your vision of change:

- provides an extensive list of every conceivable ideas for your change options
- excludes opinions about the list of ideas.

In brainstorming sessions you and your team come together and put all of your ideas together. Effective communication is one of the most effective methods when delivering a message of change to the people in your business.

The workshopping sessions are used to develop the ideas and determine which ones are feasible and includes:

- the details for your change plans
- measures of the value of each idea
- activities and action items
- commitment
- excitement and encouragement for all levels of the business involved in the workshopping session
- awareness of the effect that insecurities can have on change itself, the likely disturbance to the normal daily activities, and the general discomfort that change brings
- the cause and effect of fear of failure and resistance to change

## Making Changes Easily

Using large sheets of paper on the walls around the room to list all of the ideas allows you to review them later. Printable whiteboards are also effective, but someone should copy what's written on the whiteboards before they're erased.

Don't spend time deliberating and wondering who has the better idea. You should explain to your workshop group:

- the change idea itself
- the approach you are considering to make this change
- the policies and processes that will be used to put the change in motion
- the methods you are proposing to use
- the systems to be used
- the ideas that will work immediately and those that won't apply yet

To ensure that you have the information you need to recall the details of all the ideas later, here is a list of questions that the participants in the brainstorming session need to be thinking about during the process:

- What have you learned from your list of ideas (vision of change)?
- What are you doing now that you will continue to do?

- What will do differently going forward?
- What has no place in the future of the business?
- What actions for each of the ideas do you need to do now?

Be sure to ask yourself questions like these: What is the key to your business's being successful? What key skills do you bring to the business, and what skills do your employees bring to it? What are the main problems that you have observed in your business? What has happened in the past and what went well? What didn't go well? How do you feel about those negative experiences? What positive experiences do the stakeholders convey? What did they like about your products and services? What do they really want?

Don't forget the value of confidential surveys, as they can overcome a lot of the uncertainty associated with change projects. Independent consultants can conduct these types of surveys in order to ensure anonymity of the ideas and issues. When they gather the information and prepare a report on the comments the survey generated, you can see what you are up against before you start, as few are lucky enough to have everyone on board with change ideas from the beginning.

| Vision | Name it | Approach to be used | Process of change | Systems needed | Due Dates |
|---|---|---|---|---|---|
| Idea #1 | Change the layout of the office space | Environmentally friendly, people-friendly. Update the colour scheme | Seek expert advice for environmentally suitable ideas to improve the air flow and natural lighting options. | Additional equipment, placement of air conditioning, electrical wiring, etc. | Be realistic. Consider the employees' peak workloads. |
| Idea #2 | New printer, copier, and scanner | Location of the equipment and users' access | Seek supplier to meet the needs of workloads | Will all users be connected through a central access? Will scanned items be kept? | Date of expected delivery and training for users |

Table 3: Workshopping Action Plan

So far you have learned how to compile a list of the brainstormed ideas and a few ways to create and develop workshop action lists to work on your change ideas. The references to case studies show the effectiveness of brainstorming in resolving the complaints of dissatisfied customers. The ideas can motivate you to be more creative with your vision for change. Above all, keep asking and answering questions, even the tough questions, and remain positive and motivated throughout the workshop so you are not demotivated by negative comments from customers or your team. Utilise Table 3 as a way to start an action plan.

# CHAPTER 4

# MOTIVATION AND COMMITMENT TO CHANGE

Both the motivation to change and commitment to change are required if your plans are to be fulfilled.

## What are motivation and commitment?

Motivation is what gives you the positive energy you need to achieve your goal. Commitment is the dedication and follow-through required to achieve the goal.

What makes motivation and how can it be sustained? Being motivated does not mean you are always excited or fully committed, but it gives a person a reason to complete a set of tasks, even when those tasks are difficult, uninteresting, or just plain boring.

How would you answer these four questions?

- What motivates you to change?
- Where are you in relation to your sense of belonging and achievement?
- What would sustain your commitment to the changes you are proposing?

- How do you rate yourself when it comes to achieving positive outcomes when you want to change something? Are you strong in seeing projects to the end and achieving results, or are you average?

If you want something to change, name it, claim it, and work through it until you finish it. Choose one or a number of things that you would like to change in your business. The guidelines later in this chapter will list a series of questions to prompt your thinking on these topics.

## Negativity kills positive motivation

Positive motivation creates a positive response to what you are doing, such as enjoyment and optimism. How are you feeling right now about the activities you are about to undertake? On the other hand, negativity results in our undertaking tasks or activities with little energy and focus. The result may be seen in negative outcomes, such as failure or not finishing a task on time.

Almost everyone will experience either a positive or negative motivational experience during a change project. For example, if we don't have the right balance between our private lives and our work, times of change will make the imbalance worse. Change puts immense pressure on those on the team who may be expected to do their normal daily activities and the project tasks as well. It will mean longer hours, which can disrupt their private lives and derail their morale. Unexpected events like the failure of needed equipment to arrive can exacerbate the situation as workloads back up.

These types of situations can be frustrating and deflating to you and your team. You must sustain your motivation to return your focus to the change vision. When you feel that you are going off track, there are several ways you can kick-start your motivation again.

(1) **Step back from the situation:** A loss of motivation and inspiration for your vision may be the result of frustration that something is not happening fast enough or not at all or the feeling that "they just don't get it." If you step back from the situation, you may see that there is a good reason for something's having stalled. Taking time out from your situation to distance yourself from the problem can often do wonders for your morale.

(2) **Focus on other activities** for a while to allow your thoughts to readjust. Take a walk, play with your dog, go for a drive, exercise, or work on another office or household activity. If your waning motivation is a mental block, then doing another activity can distract the mind and give it a break until you are ready to resume the activity that stalemated the progress to being with.

You need your mind on your side to achieve positive outcomes.

(3) **Break the task into small portions:** When a task is stalled or difficult to finish, it is often because the job is too big. In this case, break the task into more manageable pieces. A daily action plan is a good way to start the day.[12] Write down a list of manageable steps you need to achieve for the day to alleviate your anxiety when you are starting to feel overwhelmed. Try to give yourself only three tasks to achieve; if that's all you do for the day, then that's three tasks achieved, and three fewer you have on your to do list. If that turns out to be way too easy, you'll likely be motivated to keep going and achieve more.

(4) **Schedule changes:** Keep variety in your schedule, and know when your energy level allows you to perform at your best. Ensure you don't undertake high-energy activities when your energy level is normally low. The drain on your natural reserves can lead to health issues.

Maximising your time by looking at the best time of day to undertake your activities is a sure way to get fired up and get things done, so make changes to your schedule to

---

[12] A Daily Action Planner is included at the back of the book. It provides space to write in all the things you need to do first, followed by the rest of the details. The Monthly Planner enlarges the approach.

match the task with the time of day. If people's schedules could be changed so they could spend more time on high-energy activities (rather than, say, meetings) when they are performing at their peak, the outcomes would be substantially improved. Doing what you enjoy first generally makes you happier, and a happier and more energised person always achieves more. To perform at your best ensure you are in a happy place before starting.

Questions that you need to ask of yourself in order to maximise your time include what time of day you work the most effectively. Use those peak times to address what you want to change. You can also make yourself look at a problem differently by changing your environment, such as by walking on a treadmill, on the beach, or in the park. A change of scenery is one way of doing one thing differently.

(5) **Rest:** To avoid losing your momentum, make time for short, planned breaks throughout the process, be it eight hours of uninterrupted sleep or a short holiday.

It's not easy to maintain motivation when you're tired and lack the necessary energy to follow through on your plans. There are ways to get your energy back and allow your mind to rest. We often forget to breathe deeply enough through the course of our day, so remember to breathe, and consider learning how to meditate. There are many meditation CDs on the market,[13] or you can take a class. Being still and listening to your own breath helps to still a racing or tired mind.

Sometimes your need for rest may be fulfilled by no more than a brief break. For some people a ten- or fifteen-minute nap refreshes and revitalises the energy levels sufficiently to undertake another task. Scientists at the Salk Institute for Biological Studies have found that "power naps can lift productivity and mood, lower stress, and improve memory and learning."

(6) **Mandatory breaks**[14]: The world won't stop spinning if you take a break. Taking time to manage your life and achieve the necessary balance between your private life and your business activities is the best gift you can give yourself and your family. Reconnect with those around you, re-energise, and nourish yourself. Go for a drive, take a one-day holiday, have a picnic at the beach. You can write your notes while you are at the beach. Short breaks are better than no breaks at all.

---

[13] Richard Latham of Meditainment has a series that is available at www.meditainment.com.

[14] The planners in the guidelines can assist here. Shade out the times set aside for yourself first, then time for the family, and then time for your work. It's the reverse, however, when you do all the things you want to first; the rest is easier. You won't be too tired to go to the gym.

I find that, when I take a short break in my busy schedule, I gain a new perspective and energy that takes me back to work re-energised. Often it's a trip to the shopping centre or to catch up with friends for coffee or a movie. Taking yourself away from the situation for a short time allows you to refocus before resuming your tasks. A trip to the beach or a park for a picnic around a scheduled meal time is another way to refresh and relax.

(7) **Keep up the momentum:** During projects of change it is practical to keep your eye on the clock and achieve a certain amount of the workload within set timeframes. By maintaining a reasonable pace during the day, you will see results. When there are interruptions to that momentum, it can take time to re-establish the pace.

When I studied art, I was fascinated with the great architects and painters, especially Michelangelo. When Sydney hosted the Olympics in 2000, I saw some of his works at an exhibition. According to the narrator of the movie at the Exhibition, whenever he was asked when it was going to be finished, he always responded, "When it's finished." It took him more than four years to complete.

This approach is an example of how some things may just take time. Looking at the ceiling today, and how much joy it continues to bring to all who have seen it over the centuries, it was worth the wait. The lesson is for you to be involved in your life and what you are doing when you are doing it.

(8) **Rewards:** Giving yourself a reward for completing a task makes a task seem much more, well, rewarding. Something as simple as a piece of chocolate or a cup of tea, a massage, or a day in the country can stimulate your senses and motivate you back into "the zone" again.

Do something different today. In fact, do something different right now. Put all of these strategies together now and see how motivated you become for the days, weeks, or months ahead when you start implementing change for you and your business.

> One very important aspect of motivation is the willingness to stop and to look at things that no one else has bothered to look at. This simple process of focusing on things that are normally taken for granted is a powerful source of creativity. —Edward de Bono[15]

---

[15] de Bono, Edward. (2000). *Six Thinking Hats: An Essential Approach to Business Management.* London, England, Penguin

## Sustaining Motivation

We all experience the tidal waves of change and the impacts of those changes at times throughout our lives. Even the most motivated employees can hit quicksand in their daily lives and businesses. As Helen Keller said, "Optimism is the faith that leads to achievement. Nothing can be done without hope and confidence."

When you begin to feel the onset of a demotivating cycle, *stop* whatever you are doing and allow yourself to refocus your mind. Being and staying motivated in times of change is challenging for most people. If you are only a visionary and don't have the tenacity and staying power for the follow-through, work with people who complement your skill set. Your wonderful ideas may remain no more than ideas if you don't apply the necessary resources to them.

## More Questions:

Now would be a good time to examine your responses to questions about how well you know yourself, your team, your change leader and team, and your employees. Write your responses down and discuss them with your team.

Come up with an action plan that breaks each step into smaller steps, ensure there is variety in your schedule of activities and action items, remember to step back from what you are doing, and take a rest break if things become overwhelming for you. Do you know how to maintain the momentum of the action items, your employees, and your ideas? Write down a list of rewards that you will be giving yourself and your employees.

When making change, we come up with numerous ways to make it happen, and we have a lot of initial motivation and excitement about the new idea. However, our motivation can change like the weather if we don't take charge of it. Sometimes we have to ask ourselves what stops us from being and staying motivated and consider how to navigate the blocks or barriers to staying motivated.

Gloria Steinem once observed that "the first problem for all of us, men and women, is not to learn, but to unlearn." Who and what we are now is a result of what we were taught and what we have experienced throughout our lives. Therefore, as Normal Vincent Peele suggested, we need to "change our thoughts to change our world."

## Energy

Our energy can be zapped easily by our fear of failure, when doubts creep in about our ability to make something happen and to sustain the activities to achieve the desired outcome. Conserving our energy is important during a change project, whether it is short or long, because it usually isn't the only thing you are working on. You may have to bounce from one thing to another quickly, which can drain your mental energy. Monitor your energy levels regularly during the change process so you don't run out of the energy you need to complete the tasks at hand.

## Guidelines for motivation and commitment

This is where you answer important questions like:

- How motivated are you?
- How committed to and focused on this change project are you?
- Do you have the ability to follow through? If not, you will need to work at sustaining your energy and positivity in order to achieve your vision. If you know that you do not have the skill set to follow through and implement the change, work with people who do.
- What are your energy levels right now?
- How much energy do you need right now?
- If you are not sure of the energy that you have and what may be need to complete the change process, then estimate what it will take to see this project through. Consider using resources like putting on extra people and using extra technology to support the team in the change process.

Table 4 can guide you through aspects of motivation: who needs it, how much they need, and what you should have when this change is being brought about.

| Physical and psychological resources | | | |
|---|---|---|---|
| How focused are you? | | | |
| How focused are your team? | | | |
| How motivated are you now? | | | |
| How motivated are your team? | | | |
| What resources do you need? | | | |
| What resources does your team need to stay motivated? | | | |
| **Idea** | **Resources: Physical/ Psychological** | **Plan** | **Timeframe** |
| Idea #1 Moving furniture | (i) Movers (ii) Getting them used to the idea | How do you make the change? | When are you going to move the furniture? |

| Idea #2 New Uniforms | (i) Contact an image specialist. (ii) Consider the wardrobe. | (i) At what point do you involve your employees? (ii) Consider their input. | Will you use the introduction of the new outfits in your marketing releases? |

Table 4: Physical and Psychological Resources

While you are continuing to ask and answer these questions, you are building the tracks on which you will place the train of change for yourself, your employees, and your business. Answer the questions, undertake the necessary research, and seek assistance from experts who can help you through the changes you have envisaged for your business. The foundation for these changes is being laid down a piece at a time. The ideas brainstormed and selected for your change process may not come to fruition without the support of your employees, so find out how they feel about this change. If you don't know the answer to that question, you may be about to find out.

# CHAPTER 5

# CHANGE HOW YOUR BUSINESS THINKS—STEP BY STEP

Do you know how your business thinks? "How it thinks" is basically the culture of the company. Do your employees know that it exists, and do they believe in it? If you are not sure or don't know, then find out. Your company's culture can create a business of choice for your customers and your employees. You want your current customers to keep coming back and new ones to consider coming on board. You need your employees to want to keep coming enthusiastically to work. What is it about your company that keeps them working with you? What services do you provide? You must know this before making changes to your business because it may be necessary to add more services for your employees or customers if the change impedes your current services.

Know your stakeholders and remind them that they are high on your agenda. Show them you can answer questions like what your customers want from your products and services, and what relationship you have established with third-party service providers. More to the point, know what your stakeholders expect of you.

Use workshops as a way to discover the effect of your business and what it means in the daily lives of your employees, customers, and other stakeholders. This type of questioning can be applied to any size business, although in larger businesses it should be considered division by division based on the number of employees who factor into the change you wish to make to the business.

All the minds of the business must be as one to effect a change. A strong company culture can help with this. Leading experts who have defined and identified features of culture include Ravasi and Schultz (2006),[16] who described organisational culture as "a set of shared mental assumptions that guide interpretation and action in organisations by defining appropriate behaviour for various situations."

## Each company has its own unique culture

Variations to the culture, no matter how slight, are impacted by the size of the company. In larger organisations diverse and even conflicting cultures can co-exist. These cultures can act contrary to the main cultural dynamic of your

---

[16] Ravasi, D., and M. Schultz. (2006). Responding to organizational identity threats: exploring the role of organizational culture. *Academy of Management Journal*, 49: 3, 433–458.

business. The culture dynamic is due to the differing characteristics of the members of the management team, their perceptions, and what they want to bring to the business. Sometimes their style can have a positive and valuable impact, but it can also create barriers to the progress of proposed changes.

## Are your change ideas being railroaded?

In your review you may even discover that the culture is being manipulated in some way. For example, a team leader may send an incomplete and unclear message to his or her team, and the distorted message may leave team members uncomfortable and resistant to aspects of the change plan. They may have their own agenda. Alternatively there may be a disgruntled employee who just isn't ever going to be on board with the changes and who talks negatively about the changes being proposed. So be alert: when you are making changes on a grand scale, the cultural dynamic—the attitudes, beliefs, and behavioural patterns that make your business what it is—may not be obvious. The cultural dynamic is reflected in your employees. It can create "stop work meetings" that slow down the progress of change, trip you up, or push your efforts off track. Identify these employees quickly. You need to know who these employees are and what they are saying and ensure that they understand the reasons for the changes you are making to the business with their help.

Do you understand the dynamic of what culture is and how powerful a tool it can be at this time of change? "Overall the organisational culture may also have varying aspects of negative and positive characteristics."[17] Schein (2009),[18] Deal and Kennedy (2000),[19] and Kotter (1992)[20] all concluded that "organisations have sub-cultures within the cultures that have their own dynamic. Culture is the organisation and vice versa. It is established by something symbolic as well as the communications it deliver as to who it is as a business." [21]Culture is basically the experience that an individual has, as well as the various perceptions that one feels when talking or speaking of an organisation. According to Kotter and Heskett, "The organisational communication perspective on culture views culture in three different ways (a) traditionalism, (b) interpretivism and (c) critical-interpretivism."[22]

---

[17] Shein, Edgar, (1992) Organisational Culture and Leadership: A Dynamic View, San Francisco, CA Jossey-Bass,

[18] Shein, Edgar. (1992). *Organizational Culture and Leadership: A Dynamic View*. San Francisco, CA: Jossey-Bass, p. 9.

[19] Deal T. E., and A. A. Kennedy. (1982). *Corporate Cultures: The Rites and Rituals of Corporate Life*. Harmondsworth: Penguin Books.

[20] Kotter, John, and James Heskett. (1992). *Corporate Culture and Performance*. Belmont, California: Free Press.

[21] Kotter, John, and James Heskett (1992) Corporate Culture and Performance, Belmont, California, Free Press.

[22] Kotter, John, and James Heskett. (1992). *Corporate Culture and Performance*. Belmont, California. Free Press.

Kotter and Heskett viewed traditionalism as seeing culture "through objective things such as stories, rituals, and symbols,"[23] interpretivism as seeing culture "through a network of shared meanings (organization members sharing subjective meanings),"[24] and critical-interpretivism as seeing culture "through a network of shared meanings as well as the power struggles created by a similar network of competing meanings."[25]

Remember the suggestion made earlier about using a confidential survey? Think beyond the survey and hold effective meetings. Think about how comprehensive your questions are going to be for both of these scenarios. You need the availability of detailed responses. Seek employees' ideas. Knowing your employees may require only that you hold a workshop on the ideas from the brainstorming session. Your observations of their interactions their involvement and buy-in may identify any potential resistance to the change ideas.

---

[23] Kotter, John, and James Heskett. (1992). *Corporate Culture and Performance*. Free Press.

[24] Kotter, John, and James Heskett. (1992). *Corporate Culture and Performance*. Free Press.

[25] Modaff, D. P., S. DeWine, and J. Butler. (2011). *Organizational communication: Foundations, challenges, and misunderstandings* (2nd ed.). Boston: Pearson Education.

## Getting to the *Business Think* stage

When you conduct a team workshop to discover what your business thinks about your ideas on change, you'll want to communicate several important points to your employees about the culture you would like to see going forward. Your action plan will involve:

- describing to your employees the type of change you are proposing;
- describing the details of the change, including the method of communication you are going to use when you explain it to your employees and when you update them later on what has been achieved and what will change next, what resources are available to you and what resources they have to achieve the goals, whether you will have a change leader from your existing employee pool or you will bring in someone from the outside, and whether the change leader will have all the necessary skills and demeanour to lead your employees through the maze of change;
- looking at your due diligence reports, the shared vision, the focus needed and the need for urgency in bringing this change about as quickly as possible;
- what your plans look like right now, using the Change Train to view one compartment at a time,

and what's in each compartment and a plan for its journey;
- describing what and who will be affected when making the change;
- your change leader and what his or her message will be to your employees.

Making your business boom requires thought as to what could make it be exceptional as a business. Think beyond the next year or two. What would you like it to look like ten years from now? Who will you have with you on this journey of change? As part of the Harvard Business Review's Advisory Council, a panel of select readers who have opted to be informed of and participate in research studies from Harvard Business Review, I have received many surveys. Through participation in their surveys, I have had regular opportunities to provide feedback and share ideas with editors and product developers across the Harvard Business Review Group. The participation has been an important learning experience and has provided an exciting preview of the lengths they go to uncover what we think. It also provides outcomes of the contributions made by all participants in helping to shape the content the Harvard Business Review develops and delivers to future customers.

How I receive information and purchases from Harvard Business Review has changed significantly over the years. They use eBooks for the iPad and PDF services on purchases, both of which save postage and provide instant results after a purchase. They also offer services for educators online and benefits for students who require course eBooks. It is amazing how far businesses can go when they ask questions of their customers in an effort to meet their needs.

## How will you achieve the *Business Think* state?

Once you have established what cultural foundation you have or want to have, relay that message to your employees. The extent of the preparation for change will depend on how developed the culture is. Ensure you have your employees on board with the change ideas.

Continue writing your notes on the ideas for change, and consider the following:

- Assess the situation, and state the obvious:
- Know where you are!
- Know where you want to go!
- Do a business review on your company; executive meetings, employee focus groups; employee surveys; benchmarking the extent of the change.
- Vision; goals; clear, quick wins; internal stakeholders; specific, measurable, SMART moves.
- What are the change and the roll-out plan?

- What will the plans look like? Have workable, achievable, and deliverable plans.
- Communicate the plan to the team.
- Implement the plan.
- Assess and use the SMART[26] technique to roll out your plans to work through goals and objectives:
- *Specific*—identify a specific area for improvement.
- *Measurable*—quantify an indicator of progress.
- *Assignable*—specify who will do it.
- *Realistic*—state what results are to be achieved, given the resources.
- *Time-related*—specify when the result(s) can be achieved."[27]

Finally, commit to the plan. Write down the details for this strategy.

## How far will you go to make a change?

What you are about to undertake will have an impact on you, your business, your employees, and the life you and your employees have come to know and enjoy. Your comfort zone is about to be redefined and redesigned,

---

[26] Doran, George T. (1981). There's a S.M.A.R.T. way to write management's goals and objectives. *Management Review* 70(11).
[27] Doran, George T. (1981). There's a S.M.A.R.T. way to write management's goals and objectives. *Management Review* 70(11).

and some may be disconcerted by the experience. Identify the change leader if you are not going to do it, how you plan to communicate the change, the project objectives, the performance, the overall approach, and the resources.

There are several steps that need to be considered before heading into the departments/divisions with your new broom. Creating a positive work environment is the foundation of employee engagement. Business leaders typically don't engage employees, but they can create an environment that will encourage employees to engage. The environment itself also has to be engaging. Motivate for high performance and a culture of recognition.

## Have you described the change you want?

Describe the change you hope to achieve clearly. Visualising what you hope to achieve and conveying it are two different things. Write down what it is you want to change. Then talk to a mentor or a trusted friend about what you want to change. Talk as if you have already achieved the change, and consider the control you may or may not have and who will be doing the influencing. When it comes to the mechanics of the proposed changes you are about to initiate, there are several important considerations.

## You need detail when planning change

Write down the critical components for the success of the change you are proposing. The more detailed your understanding and delivery are, the better the outcome will be. Consider:

- the communication method you will use
- what resources are available to you
- the leadership style required

A number of details are important for communicating your message:

- What are you going to add to the business?
- Is it technology, a new location, new products, new services?
- How are you going to communicate the right message to your employees or team?
- How involved will you be in the process?
- Who else should be involved in this change process?
- What should be done about any possible resistance to change? Do you have a plan to deal with resistance? Do you have answers to all the possible resistance-to-change questions participants may have?
- Who is going to lead the change? Who will be the champion of change?

There are three more important matters to consider when implementing changes:

- the *what* factor
- the plan
- the reward (which is how to make change as painless as possible)

## The *what* factor

*What* do you need to make happen? Your employees and other resources are essential. *What* do you have already, and *what* do you need to have to see the amber light turn to green? *What* sort of training is required? *What* timeframe is required to complete the training? *What* personnel need this training? *What* attitude do these employees have that may need to be changed beforehand or along the way? *What* changes do you need to make yourself?

For the plan and reward phases of the change, you'll want to make change painless and as stress-free and confusion-free as possible. Offset the possible angst and aggravations that go with change. What will you offer for this discomfort? How will you keep you employees interested and motivated? Can you have Friday lunches delivered to the office? Would a Wednesday afternoon ice cream break reward your staff?

What steps can you take to make the change painless or at least less painful? Plan the party now. Let them know the date, the time, the place, what they are required to do, and what they can expect. How will you acknowledge them for all their efforts for the change?

## The execution of change

You can execute in two ways: Succeed swiftly and some feathers may fly, or succeed gradually and win them all over during the process. The latter change will be far more effective, as the change will become embedded into the culture. Consider the following pragmatic steps:

- Analyse the organisation's current position and the need for change through due diligence.
- Ensure that the vision and the direction of the company are shared.
- Stay focused on the present.
- Create a sense of urgency about how, what, when, why, and so on.
- Demonstrate strong leadership in the change process.
- Prepare an effective plan that can be implemented and that involves strategic employees.
- Communicate effectively with the employees throughout the process.
- Follow up the vision and strategy often.

## The importance of planning

Planning ensures all of your ideas come to fruition. Planning is the second most powerful component of the Change Train.[28] Someone, somewhere, somehow will be affected, so you must take responsibility. Individuals or business managers can design the change to ensure success is in the details so the change can be implemented successfully. How do you ensure a positive reaction to the proposed change? Know and understand the stakeholders so you can focus on who and what needs to change. Then take action on those changes, and keep your employees positive, on track, motivated, focused, and happy during the transition you initiate.

## Making change happen

Ensure that your process is shaped and fitted to your business change ideas, or managing the change will be ineffectual. The type of change you are proposing and who will be affected are two focal points of making change. For example, you must consider how the change affects the stakeholders as well as your company's culture, as "Corporate Culture can have a significant impact on a firm's long-term economic performance."[29]

---

[28] Change Train™ is the time2manage seminar method.
[29] Kotter, John, and James Heskett. (1992). *Corporate Culture and Performance*. Belmont, California: Free Press.

How does your business move? Is it large like a large bulk carrier container—slow to get started, able to take the rough weather, and too big to slow down or adapt quickly—or as sleek as a speed boat that can skim through the water in normal weather but has some difficulty when things get rough and can flip at any time? How is your organisation built? Is your business in a constant state of flux right now? At this point, ensure that your approach to making change matches the initiatives you will be introducing and applying to bring about change.

## Who will lead the change?

The qualities of your change leader must include their ability to be proactive and visible when the change is being undertaken. He or she needs the authority to make it happen. As Goethe said, "Behaviour is the mirror in which everyone shows their image." The change leader should be seen as someone who can make something happen and who proactively participates in making the change idea move effectively. This kind of behaviour will be reflected in the positive responses you receive or in the resistance you experience when the call goes out to the business and the personnel to implement the change.

Three components make a good change leader:

- Visibility—Employees will rely on the visibility of the change leader in the organisation on as a barometer for the entire process.
- Effective communication—The effectiveness of all communication from the start to the finish of your change management project must be consistent.
- Reliable reporting—The rapport that the change person establishes and demonstrates with others in the organisation needs to be visible and positive. Effective communication is beneficial for the effective traction of the ideas and the expected outcomes from the changes being implemented.

The change leader and the company's managers play vital roles in your process of change. Buy-in at the top provides a level of commitment when management has a clear understanding of the strategy, and everyone understands that the change is going to happen now and not just when time permits. This commitment requires that you have the capacity for the change to happen, as it may impact costs, schedules, paperwork, or results. Identifying a link between what you have now and what you will have when the change is implemented helps you to:

- assess and prioritise your options for all the ideas generated

- understand how the change affects your business and its operations and whether there are any organisational changes needed initially
- provide support for management to allow them to implement the changes. Getting some quick wins on the board is usually a great start for any project.

A successful outcome is reliant on the amount of support you receive from your teams in relation to your change ideas. Their visibility, their message, their behaviour, and their responses all have an effect on employees.

In large organisations the change leader must be supported by the other managers in order to manage resistance during the process. The managers' relationships with their team members and the effectiveness of their communication can make the difference between total success and an average/lukewarm response from other participants.

The issue of managing resistance must be addressed substantially at the beginning of the process as well as throughout the change project. As part of your set-up plan, consider and counteract any possible negativity or resistance to change, and have answers to all possible resistance-related questions. For example, prepare answers to "frequently asked questions to answer employees' questions and alleviate their fear of or doubts about the change. Anticipate what they could be thinking or feeling at this time and be prepared with adequate answers. At the end of the day, it is all about being prepared for potential road blocks and speed bumps in order to achieve the changes one issue at a time. A regular in-house newsletter that updates everyone on the progress of each phase is always helpful. Interview members of the project team, and use their comments in the newsletter. When you achieve your changes, and your team adapts to them, you'll have a winning result. Therefore, think through each step and how you will know whether the project is achieving its goals. Surveys sometimes work, as will a simple walk around the office and asking how your employees are doing with the change.

The real prize in achieving change will be whether there is traction for the changes implemented and whether those changes remain in place. If the team reverts back to the old way, then the change hasn't been successful. Therefore a "post-change" plan must include follow-ups with participants and refresher training in the new way.

If you haven't seen the television programme *Undercover Boss*, I recommend that you catch one of the programmes. The CEO in one episode took a risk to go to the stores that were making progress as well as those that were not performing. The CEO listened to the workers and was happy to support them in their suggestions. When you listen to your employees, there can be no better advocate than that employee in bringing about the change that they want. Reward and recognition is beneficial and generally motivates other workers to put forward their ideas too. The businesses featured on *Undercover Boss* are not different from yours in that the CEOs know that some things need to change and that ground level is the perfect starting point. Even if you are a small business, asking some hard questions and being prepared to listen and consider suggestions may be the first step to letting go of an old way of doing things and bringing about a fresh change to your business. The experience of "going undercover" can open up new opportunities for growth and improvement.

## Due diligence data

Due diligence, planning, and ensuring you have the necessary resources must be done before implementing a change in ideas. When you are proposing growth in your business, go beyond the numbers. In your due diligence, look at your company's financial and non-financial targets in order to understand the larger context of the business and identify potential problems or areas that may impact your business's position overall. Consider the product, the services, and the stakeholders in your due diligence, and review the financial implications of your proposed change strategy by analysing your projections. The projections should include your strategy and company structure and identify whether they are capable of dealing with the change. Review the change in the business approach from the risk, commercial, revenue, and tax perspectives.

You may relate to a case study on Anglo American, one of the world's largest mining companies, in *Adding Value through Asset Optimisation*, no matter how large or small your business. Not every company is as large as Anglo American, but the approach is realistic, and it achieved resounding success worldwide. How they viewed their ability to optimise their business contains some important considerations.

Anglo American operates in Africa, Europe, South America, North America, Australia, and Asia. Its portfolio is a mix of mining businesses and natural resources, and it employs approximately 100,000 people. Its operating profit in 2010 was almost $10 billion.

Through their approach of asset optimisation, Anglo-American has become performance-oriented, focusing changes on:

- being the employer of choice by encouraging employees to step forward with initiatives to improve the business
- being an investment partner because of their asset value

- skills development, mindsets, and behaviours
- being performance-driven through cost and productivity improvements

How they achieved their goal of asset optimisation on such a grand scale involved the design of their plan, testing the plan in one area of the organisation, and including the change in the day-to-day operations.

These three efforts have placed Anglo American's operations among the most efficient. The asset optimisation concept unlocks the value of resources and employees, establishes and improves the business culture, and implements improvements across the business that are suggested by customers as well as by all divisions and operations.

The company's asset optimisation is linked closely to the Japanese concept of *Kaizen* or continuous improvement, which challenges all employees to make ongoing improvements to the quality of their work. Employees are empowered to make decisions that affect the quality of products and services across the organisation, resulting in cost reductions, less waste, and satisfaction in achieving the best results.

Like many efforts, asset optimisation requires communication, learning and skill development, and developing available opportunities.

## Making Changes Easily

The process sets a clear view of how operational improvement can be planned by identifying an opportunity for improvement and putting it into practice. By setting challenging, achievable, measurable, and visible goals with your existing resources and capacities, you will see a shift in your change process. When diverse teams with different skills and specialisations share their ideas or offer solutions amazing things can be achieved.

You see, once the Change Train starts moving, it can achieve success for you and your business. Anglo American used newsletters, posters, and more to report on success stories and drive the message across the organisation.

Work closely with your finance employees, whether it's your own small business accountant or your finance manager if you have a larger organisation. The information gleaned from financial reviews should include data about income and IT facilities to allow for a smooth transition to your strategic position. The time period for an effective review does vary from situation to situation. Therefore it is prudent to build due diligence it into every major project transaction. Ask yourself the following questions:

1. What are the monetary transactions likely to be in this change process? What is the extent of your investment for this change? What are the key drivers for the change?

2. What are the specific risks in making this change happen? What strategy have you considered to ensure that there is the requisite focus on and tailoring of the change procedures that will be included in this change project?
3. How will you manage all requests for information on the change process? Who in management will work with you to establish a significant and robust plan that is suitable for the changes proposed?
4. Who will prepare detailed procedures for the change project? Does the preparation for the change strategy include detailed financial analyses and discussions with management as to when and where their input is required?
5. Does your strategy include real-time updates? Who will review, consider, and deliver the findings from surveys and reports to ensure that management and the participants are aware of all issues raised through the phases of the change project? Will the stakeholders have confidence in the ongoing reports and the final outcome?

Ensure that you undertake a rigorous due diligence process or the changes may not be as effective as you had hoped. Now more than ever, an effective and comprehensive due diligence process has the capacity to mitigate organisational, reputational, and financial risks during the day-to-day business. Being a savvy leader, no matter the size of the organisation or the transaction, requires that you use experienced employees to undertake the due diligence. They need to produce a report that allows you to execute a smooth transition for successful growth.

The due diligence report should include full information and the development in regard to:

- the change management process
- the dynamics that bring about effective change
- understanding and clarifying mutual expectations
- detailing all of the costs involved in the project
- the time involved,
- the employees who should participate and be part of the change team

Ensure that the person who is going to lead the change project has agreed to the expectations you and your trusted advisors have outlined and that he or she selects the right dynamic for the change team participants. Consider whether individuals get along, what types of mechanisms are to be used, and the level of reporting that you expect and require to allow effective decision-making processes. There will always be room for improvement, but the leader needs to be convinced that what is proposed will work. Take a fresh look at what is being proposed by workshopping the idea(s).

When you undertake the workshopping session, include innovative concepts broken down into small segments to allow the project to work effectively. Always be alert for any negative effects, such as outsourcing, that may affect those in the business if they are not considered. Ensure that each step of the project is analysed in terms of the tasks involved in the project. Consider using project management tools, flow charts, and risk factors, and include the impact of time delays in the deliverable timeframes. Outline what can be tolerated and what cannot to establish the project's boundaries. Get to know your employees (if you don't already) at the workshopping phase of the project idea.

You can expect that some employees will need more direction than others, organisations' personality dynamics differ, employees' priorities and motivations differ based on their needs for the change being proposed, and employees' strengths and weaknesses differ. Other considerations will depend on the type of business that you are proposing to change. If you use a survey, make sure that the participants have the opportunity to respond with details and examples regarding the changes you are proposing, rather than yes-or-no responses. For example, if you are considering moving furniture around the office, show them the design options that you have sourced from the designers and give them a choice in the change process. Offer colour palates and options available, as going with the majority vote is more likely to win the change vote than the minority.

However, if there are no options as to colour and layout, then explain in detail the reasoning behind why you want to make the changes you are proposing.

In circumstances where you are proposing to change one aspect of your company's image by, for example, changing or introducing uniforms may be a positive move for your business. Judith Rasband, Conselle L.C. president and CEO and director of the Conselle Institute of Image Management, said, "The way we dress affects the way we *think*, the way we *feel*, the way we *act* and the way that others *react* to us." For instance, you may want the uniform to send the right message about you, your company and its services. Professional image and business etiquette consultant Debbie Whittle's mantra is "Change your image, change your life"[30] because this is exactly what happened to her. Debbie had one consultation with an image consultant that changed her life. Debbie wanted who she was on the inside reflected on the outside. After her image consultation, Debbie felt confident for the first time in her life. "Confidence," she said, "is the most powerful tool we have at our disposal and unfortunately many people have either lost confidence or never really felt that they had it."[31]

---

[30] www.t-image.com.au;
www.facebook.com/Total-Image-Consulting.

[31] www.t-image.com.au;
www.facebook.com/Total-Image-Consulting.

The challenge of change includes creative ideas to ensure a smooth transition when making change. For example, if your change plan is to moving your office, then there are several things you can do to ease the discomfort of the move for your employees. You can also offer your employees a choice of dates or days of the month for the changes to take place to overcome interruptions in their day-to-day activities, annual leave. Also you could provide them with a moving box with their name on it so they can put their desk items into a box and be ready for the movers who will be in the office on the weekend and will move the boxes for them.

When executing the change, revisit the due diligence reports that cover your vision. If there is a need for urgency in bringing about the change, be swift and supportive. With the survey results in and the plans and colours decided, tell your employees what the outcome will be and when it will happen, and clearly communicate how it will affect them so they are prepared.

Remember the reference to the Change Train™, where the train is made up of a number of compartments (similar to business divisions), and as it moves from station to station, some employees alight, and others come on board. When making changes one compartment at a time, as Anglo American did by doing a test pilot, you or your change leader should tell your employees what will be affected when the changes occur. What will the message to your employees be? Remember those three overriding considerations: visibility, the communication method, and the reporting that will ensure that the change occurs.

In an interview about her workshop strategy for making corporate image changes, Debbie Whittle said that she challenges her participants "to step out of their comfort zone and to really have a conversation with themselves about where they see themselves. This is very important in a business situation." Whittle added that one topic that intrigues employees is finding out "what people are saying behind your back" and how we are perceived during the change project. If you wish to succeed in business, you must be aware of your own strengths and showcase them because, as Whittle said, "Making the decision to find out and to possibly change how we are perceived can literally be life changing."

Your business change can succeed and be exceptional when you include all of these features. Think beyond the next year or two. How would you like your business to look in ten years' time? Who will you have with you? Include your responses in your guidance notes to remind yourself of issues you need to consider.

Your strategy for change requires that you keep making changes and acting on them. Assessing the situation is stating the obvious, of course, but it will help you achieve your vision about where you want to end up, similar to a health check: Know where you are at now and along the way. Know where you want to go! Know the condition your company is in. Include these requirements in the brainstorming session, the workshopping session, the due diligence review, the follow-ups on the ideas, and executive meetings in order to revisit continuously the positions of the benchmarks you have set.

Ensure your goals have plans behind them that include the roll-out of the phases of the project. When implementing your plan, include the same detail and precision in order to achieve a successful outcome. When assessing the plan for the roll-out of the changes, use the "SMART" technique. Your own commitment to the plan as well as the commitment of those asked to participate will create the results you are looking for. Here are some of the questions you need to answer as part of your due diligence.

| Questions | Your Responses | Change Team Participants' Responses |
|---|---|---|
| How will you stay motivated? How are you going to persuade them? How are you planning to deliver your change plan? | | |

## Making Changes Easily

| | | |
|---|---|---|
| Description of your strategy: use bullet points or write at least 100 words. | | |
| | | |
| What and who do you involve:<br>(a) a division?<br>(b) the whole company?<br>(c) due diligence specialists/professionals, specialist change managers | | |
| Clearly describe:<br>(a) what communication method you will use<br>(b) What resources you need (employees, equipment, money)<br>(c) what the management style will be:<br>  1. What are the styles of your participants? If you don't know, find out before putting the plan into action.<br>  2. Plan the Change Train. | | |

Table 5: Due Diligence Factors

# CHAPTER 6

# PRINCIPLES FOR PLANNING CHANGE—JUST THE BASICS

First comes thought; then organization of that thought into ideas and plans; then transformation of those plans into reality. The beginning, as you will observe, is in your imagination. —Napoleon Hill, the Founder of the Science of Success.

## The basics of the modern principles of change management

Numerous books have been written on the subject of change, including *Harvard Business Review on Change* by Richard Pascale, *Leading Change* by John P. Kotter, and *Agile Change Management: a practical framework for successful change planning and implementation* by Melanie Franklin. If you want to delve into the theory of change in depth, read as much as you want in order to achieve your goals. Some basic principles will hold you in good stead as you commence this change process:

- Use effective management.
- Know what change means to you, what has to change and why.

## Making Changes Easily

- Anticipate what can go wrong and why.
- Visualise your business moving from its current position to booming with the changes you implement.
- Identify when and how you will reward the participants when the change has been made.

Before we go further, let's remember what change means. The Macquarie dictionary describes the process of change as "to make different, to substitute another or others for something; exchange for something else; give and take, to remove and replace; move in a different direction…"

For the purposes of this exercise, if we look at change as a train, it helps us see our change ideas differently. What do we think of and what do we see when we picture the change as part of a Change Train? There are a number of carriages, and the choice you make when choosing the carriage you sit in could be for a particular reason or a subconscious decision.

The sub-consciousness of our decision to sit in the designated carriage will stem from our supporting our own needs first. It may be the carriage that has Wi-Fi, the one in which there is no conversation allowed so you can work uninterrupted, the first carriage, or the last carriage. Whatever the carriage, there is a choice involved. If you were in a car instead, and you were not the driver, you would usually have a preference as to where you would like to sit—the front passenger seat, the back seat driver's side, or the back seat passenger side.

The concept of train carriages can also be likened to an organisation's divisions/departments, to your family, and to your social groups. The carriages contain people from various locations who have been picked up along the way. Change is always on the move. The train can stop along its route, pick up more people, and drop some off. It can move forward, reverse, go off the tracks, stop at one location for too long, and make unscheduled stops, all for a variety of reasons. Therefore, whether scheduled or unscheduled, there will be delays in arriving at your destination.

What affects the carriages of the train? It's usually the people in them, their behaviour and attitudes, but they can also be affected by the weather, the time of year, the temperature in the carriage, and the unscheduled stops.

What do we have to contend with when considering change implementation?

## Change principles and practices

How do you include these principles and practices when shaping your change plans? A considerable number of change management principles and rules are available, but only a few have been addressed in this book, such as the level of skill the leader, communicator, and motivator of the change team and your employees must have. In keeping the change process simple, what are the basics when it comes to prompting change in your business?

- What are the common denominators (ideas) that you and your brainstorming team came up with?
- What is the business's current position? Are you going to spruce up the business processes, allowing it to shed some deadwood and expand?
- What can we do to make to changes to? Why do you want this change? When you want it to happen? Who will make it happen? How will you make it happen, and how will you communicate the changes to your employees? Where will we make it happen? Ask yourself more questions if you need to.

At the end of several chapters you will find a table with a series of questions in the tables. Once you have answered the questions, look at any ideas you may have and at the ideas of the participants. Would they be useful here, and could the ideas be included in your plan?

## Principles of change are in themselves a discipline

Preparation starts with the individual(s) and the teams involved before the company itself changes as a whole. As the owner of the business, the manager of the business/

division, or a team leader, are you ready? Are you a good leader, communicator, and organiser who is motivated and creative? Make a list:

- What are the skills of a good leader/guide?
- What are the skills of a good communicator?
- What are the skills of a good planner and organiser?
- Are you motivated to see it through?
- How committed are you?
- How creative are you when it comes to making change?

| Question | You | Name of Change Leader: | Person #1 etc. |
|---|---|---|---|
| What skills are required to guide the changes? | | | |
| What communication skills are required? | | | |
| What plans are to be put in place? | | | |
| Who is the best planner of those on this list? | | | |
| On a scale of 1 to 10 (with 1 being the lowest), who is the most motivated? | | | |

| How creative are the participants? (Use the 1–10 scale to answer this question.) | | | |
|---|---|---|---|

Table 6: Evaluation of Skill Set

Four aspects of employees' personalities are often overlooked when preparing to make change: behaviours, attitudes, beliefs structures and motivation. According to William James, who received his doctorate from Harvard and taught psychology there beginning in 1875, "It is our attitude at the beginning of a difficult task which, more than anything else, will affect its successful outcome."

| Topic | Your comments | **Your team's comments** on how they see you in these circumstances. All team members should write down how they describe themselves on the four topics. |
|---|---|---|
| Behaviour | What are your behaviours in times of change? | |
| Attitude | What are your attitudes when someone suggests making change in your life in your daily activities at work or home? | |

| Beliefs | What are your beliefs about change? | |
|---|---|---|
| Motivation | How motivated are you right now? How motivated do you think you need to be to make changes? | |

Table 7: Behaviours, Attitudes, Beliefs, and Motivations Questionnaire

Check that you have reviewed your behaviours, attitudes, beliefs, and motivation. Ask someone on your team to give you a general critique on how they see you in each of these areas. It can be your own partner, your teammate or someone else whose opinion you value and who will respond objectively. Some of the responses may not be favourable, but they will establish their perceptions of you in relation to the change process.

## Behaviours

Many behaviours surface in the normal course of our daily lives and should be considered throughout any process of change. Behaviours are connected to attitudes, beliefs, and what motivates people. The interrelationship of these facets of personality requires your consideration and anticipation. Your employees' reactions to the change idea(s) you put forward should be the focus of your attention. Are you aware of your employees' attitudes, beliefs, and behaviours in times of change? Have you anticipated how they will react when you tell them about your plans for your vision for change? As Anthony Robbins, author of *Awaken the Giant Within* observed, "Beliefs have the power to create and the power to destroy. Human beings have the awesome ability to take any experience of their lives and create a meaning that disempowers them or one that can literally save their lives."[32]

**Attitudes**: Attitudes refer to what you like and what you don't like. The Macquarie dictionary defines attitudes as "position, disposition or manner with regard to a person or thing". While the definition is helpful, most social psychologists agree that attitude involves inclinations and predispositions, as well as whether an individual is prepared to accept change.

Attitudes are often based on our knowledge/beliefs and how emotionally attached we are to those beliefs. Because of attitudes, you may experience more or less keenness, enthusiasm, and excitement for your ideas of change and more or less support and encouragement for your change ideas. If you don't see these attitudes, part of your pitch to your stakeholders should be an effort to draw out their best qualities for the change process as

---

[32] Robbins, Anthony. (2001). *Awaken the Giant Within*. New York USA Simon & Schuster.

well as your own. When employees participate and their ideas are considered or used, then the outcomes are likely to be positive.

## Beliefs

The Macquarie Dictionary's definition of a belief is "that which is believed, an accepted opinion, conviction of the truly or reality of a thing, based upon grounds, confidence, faith, trust." As much as attitudes can be a stumbling block, you must also consider cultural circumstance, belief structures and their integration into the change project; the goals and expectations of individuals involved in the process; your and other stakeholders' self-esteem; what the stakeholders want to get out of the change project; and the need for networking with your employees across other teams as well as across the wider community where your business actions could have an impact.

## Motivation

Staying positive is difficult enough with the normal daily pressures, but coupled with a change project, it is even harder. You need to be prepared so you don't go off track in an interim stage of making your business change. How do you keep yourself and everyone positive, productive, and focused on the end goal? You must ensure that you create a positive environment during the change process and remain calm. You must also anticipate negativity and be prepared for such delays. Finally, remain positive, and handle issues that arise by using a solutions-based approach wherever possible.

If you know your employees well, consider articulating how likely each employee is to behave in the face of change? Where you are unsure of how effective your team members will be in a project situation you can undertake behavioural assessments beforehand and this will give you a better idea of the blend of the team participants you are proposing to put together.

The Beilben trainers and consultants,[33] who undertake employee assessments and provide reports for employers, commented, "During the course of the change you need to enable individuals and teams to communicate and work together with greater understanding.[34] Profile assessments and exercises developed by psychologists can identify individuals' behavioural attributes, belief structures, attitudes, and motivational drivers. The results will provide insights and an inventory of how others see themselves and others.

---

[33] www.beilben.com.

[34] www.beilben.com. Their trainers and consultants provide reports on individuals and on the compatibility of groups that you may propose using in a project environment.

The assessment results will provide detailed advice that relates to both the individuals and to the team. This strategy will help you to build productive working relationships, select and develop high-performing teams, raise self-awareness and personal effectiveness, and build mutual trust and understanding. If you want to identify team members who want to understand their contributions to the team as a whole and increase their self-awareness, there are even more specific assessments that will demonstrate your participants' strengths and allowable weaknesses, leading to better results and increased effectiveness throughout the change process.

If you do not undertake formal assessments because you are comfortable with your colleagues, you can still undertake your own enquiries into your own attitude by asking several people to comment on what they see as to your behaviours, attitudes, beliefs, and motivation overall.

## Qualities of Change Leaders

Smart leaders communicate, compensate, and commemorate achievements. Don't sit in your office and send out emails: Walk around, reach out to your employees personally, and use the phone if they work at a remote location to personalise your relationships. Coach your managers to lead. Ask your employees about what is going on and do more listening than talking.

## Making Changes Easily

In times of change, communicate early and often about what you plan to do. Include all of your stakeholders, as they may need to make changes of their own in contemplation of your proposed change. This approach leads to excellent customer service and increases trust and confidence. Leverage technology to enhance ongoing communication through electronic newsletters, webinars, podcast updates, and blogs that contain meaningful communication. This kind of communication stimulates sales and sustains interest.

Feedback is central to the success of any change project. Use Table 8 and exchange the lists among the participants. Communicate the progress of change as an important component of delivering the message of change. Always seek good counsel from people inside and outside your organisation to manage change through good feedback about the changes proposed.

While you must focus positively on your goals, you must also consider the negatives in any project. Be on the alert for saboteurs, and work to gain their co-operation by helping them overcome their fears about the change. Whom will you ask inside the business to give genuine feedback on the changes? Whom will you ask to assist you outside the business? For example as CEO, you may be part of the Association of Chief Executives or Directors and Officers Association. These platforms may be invaluable as a way to bounce ideas off other experienced businesspeople. When delivering change, use change highlights, including communicating the benefits of the change, preparing responses for the questions that may come up, demonstrating how the advantages overcome the disadvantages, and keeping the stakeholders informed.

Making changes successfully requires that you know what you need to know. Undertaking due diligence of the activities in both your work and your private life during a change phase at work will be beneficial. The daily and weekly planners provided in this book will assist you in planning your day and your week. The daily planner is a one-page list of all the things you need to do today, where the number-one item on the list is the highest importance. The weekly planner gives you an overview of the week and illustrates the importance of meeting deadlines during the week. I always encourage people to put all the activities that they want to achieve on the weekly planner, using a balance of work, rest, and play. Share your experiences and outcomes with your change team.

## Communicate the Change

If you are not in a position to test the change approach, involve everyone possible. In large organisations you may need to stagger the change across divisions and branches of the business. Know where the business is now, as

## Making Changes Easily

opposed to where you want to be in a month or three months' time. What do you want? When do you want it? Why do you want it? What you have to do to get it? That is why you must do development planning and make all plans measurable. Again, there's the common denominator of communication.

Communication involves your employees, your business, your confidence, your products, your services, your life, your family. People will always be part of everything, so there will always be a social component throughout the change process.

During your change project you need employees' skills to achieve your goals and plans, so express yourself in such a way that the employees you address understand your message. If you haven't already developed meaningful relationships in your business or social groups, there is no better time than during a change project.

Effective communication is the thread that weaves in and out among all the components of your plans. It must occur at the beginning of the change process to allow behaviours to change appropriately, and continuously providing important updates creates milestones throughout the entire process.

Goethe said, "Behaviour is a mirror in which everyone displays his image." The foundations of understanding what has been communicated depend on whether you are passive, assertive, or aggressive in your behaviour. Dr Andrew Salter[35] defined an assertive persons as "direct, responding outwardly to his environment. When confronted with a problem he takes immediate constructive action. He sincerely likes *people*, but he does not care what they may think. He makes rapid decisions, and likes responsibility. Above all, the [assertive] person is free of anxiety."[36]

Today, more than ever, it is important to be assertive in your behaviour in business. Assertive people value everyone's needs, not just their own. If you don't know how to communicate effectively in a style that is comfortable for you, knowing about the concepts of sender vs receiver and intention vs outcome may be of help:

- Where the message for the sender and receiver are the same, then the encoding (what the sender says) and decoding (what the receiver understands) will be the same.

---

[35] Dr Andrew Salter was the founder of Conditioned Reflex Therapy, an early form of behaviour therapy that emphasised assertive and expressive behaviour as the way to combat the inhibitory personality traits that Salter believed were the underlying cause of most neuroses.

[36] Price, Carol. (1994). *Assertive Communication Skills for Professionals*. Audio Workbook. CareerTrack Inc.

- When the intent of a communication doesn't deliver the desired outcome (the receiver's understanding), there may be issues in the sender's encoding or the receiver's decoding.

There are usually two people involved in communication: the sender and the receiver. When the sender sends a message, the information in that message includes the sender's attempt to encode his or her intention based on the sender's previous experience when communicating. When the receiver receives the message, he or she attempts to "decode" the message based on previous experience. When the sender's and the receiver's experiences differ, it is likely that the message will be misinterpreted. When I was in school, we played a game in which the teacher whispered a few sentences to one student in the classroom, who whispered the story to the next person. The last person in the class to receive the message told it to the class. Then the teacher read out the message he or she had told the first student. Somewhere along the whispers, the story was either misinterpreted or intentionally added to so the ending communication was usually substantially different from the beginning communication. This simple game exemplifies how people communicate with one another. You may be listening, but what are you hearing?

If sometimes the voice with which you speak to yourself is not positive all the time, then your employees are likely to be experiencing much of the same hollowness in the words you speak aloud. Your own inner self-talk is likely to affect what you are about to undertake and how you approach situations during the course of the change project.

When the receiver of the message receives the information, the message may be different from what the sender intended. Therefore, as the sender of the message, you can't always control how the message is interpreted. However, if you use certain methods of communication, you will enhance your chances of achieving a positive outcome that is consistent with the intention of your message. A change newsletter or a list of answers to frequently asked questions are effective ways to provide the right information about the change you are making because you are in control of the message that is delivered to your organisation.

When providing information about the change to your employees, consider the following questions to improve the message and communication of the change:

- Have you ever thought that you were communicating effectively and later learned that you were perceived in a completely different way than you intended?
- Have you ever asked a question at a meeting and then felt the question wasn't answered or

that it elicited an emotional response you didn't understand?
- Have you ever told someone that his or her idea wasn't important or useful and later felt you should have thought twice about doing that?
- Do you become defensive about your ideas or point of view when someone questions them?
- Do you see yourself as cool and calm, but you're very tired at the end of the day?
- Are you the one that has the bright idea that seems to solve a problem but it's seldom accepted by others?

You may have experienced one or all of these situations at one time or another. They—and similar situations—can provide insights for you to work on. We need to be:

- role models
- equally attentive and receptive to the needs of the people we work with during the change process
- participative and engaging in our communications
- co-operative and considerate in our relationships
- capable of preparing, delivering, and receiving practical and effective feedback (we need it but don't really like it)
- positive and nurturing of all involved in the change process

Your aim during this change process is to encourage, empower, and ensure that, regardless of any negativity individuals may have experienced previously, this change event will be positive for them and that they will be glad that they participate with the changes you are proposing. There will always be discomfort in times of change. (Try putting your socks on left/right foot first for a week if you usually put them on right/left foot first, and see how that simple change makes you feel.) Leading by example facilitates making change. As Henry David Thoreau said, "Live your beliefs and you can turn the world around."

If you are not going to lead the change yourself, then choose your change leader wisely. To be effective the change must be well planned and received and delivered well. Brian Tracy, a professional speaker and best-selling author, explains it simply: "Just as your car runs more smoothly and requires less energy to go faster and farther when the wheels are in perfect alignment, you perform better when your thoughts, feelings, emotions, goals and values are in balance."[37]

---

[37] Tracy, Brian. (1993). *Maximum Achievement*, New York, USA, Simon and Schuster

## Making Changes Easily

| Name | What | Why | Where | How | Who | When | Attitude | Belief | Behaviours |
|---|---|---|---|---|---|---|---|---|---|
| You | New product | Increase revenue | Across the business | All at once | All managers to lead their teams toward the common goal | By end of fiscal year | Motivated | The changes will work | focused |
| Person #1 | How does this product look? | How much money is the CEO expecting? | Sales team | Segment the demographic for delivery | All managers to play their part | Realistic deadline | Interested, motivated; probably about time | The change has potential. | Interested, not sure of the plan |
| #2 | What do they want now? We have a great product! | We are pushing a good product; maybe we need to look at a different advertising campaign. | Marketing's problem | Our team has been overloaded for the last 6–12 months. | Senior managers and the executives can do the hard work. | Longer timeframe so we can achieve it | Interested but not that interested | Any change is a good change but not right now. | Not that interested |
| #3 | | | | | | | | | |
| #4 | | | | | | | | | |

Table 8: Attitude, Belief, Behaviour Tracker

## Changes for You

You must quantify the degree to which the change is essential to you personally. Table 8 gives examples of possible responses from members of the team. What effect it will have on you if it doesn't happen? How will you react to the new way of doing things? What will your attitude and behaviour be? How organised and personally well-managed are you? How effective are your relationships and ability to communicate with others? Understand your own style, personality type, and ability to achieve goals. It you haven't examined these factors, it may be time to undergo a corporate assessment. There are a number of techniques, such as the Myers Briggs and Belbin techniques, that you may want to explore to understand your business style.

According to Michael A Robert, author of *Transformational Leadership: How Leaders Change Teams, Companies and Organisations*, "Understanding the great psychological mechanisms that cause people to resist change is important for leaders. Scholars have begun to recognise typical patterns of behaviour in response to change."[38] Dr R. M. Belbin observes that "a team is not a bunch of people with job titles, but a congregation of individuals, each of

---

[38] Robert, Michael A. (2012). *Transformational Leadership: How Leaders Change Teams, Companies and Organisations*. Chantilly Virginia, USA The Teaching Company.

whom has a role which is understood by other members. Members of a team seek out certain roles and they perform most effectively in the ones that are most natural to them."[39] It is not essential that you undertake training to learn the business styles of everyone on your team unless you have the resources, but some styles are manager, organiser, innovator, producer, presenter, counsellor, communicator, and reformer. If you undertake assessments, you will understand your strengths and what you need to develop as a leader. People are either self-motivated or other-motivated and are likely to be a combination of styles and a mix of the thinking and feeling types. By knowing this information, you identify their level of commitment, style, the path that they are likely to take in a change project, and what you will be up against. However, people differ, and anticipation of their business styles in this situation may affect the Change Train™ and its ability to arrive at the station on time! According to Meredith Belbin, teams have "a tendency to behave, contribute and interrelate with others in a particular way."[40]

## Team Dynamics

Different business styles, strengths, weaknesses, and qualities make up the dynamic of the team that you are

---

[39] www.belbin.com.
[40] www.belbin.com.

about to challenge to change. If there are weaknesses, you can support them with resources that would help them achieve the goal, as your support will come back tenfold in what they do. Take care of your employees, and they will likely take care of you and support your changes. Be mindful of their personal situations before taking them on a change journey, as the more respect you demonstrate as part of the preparation process, the more likely they will be prepared to join you on the change project. You need to consider others as much as you consider yourself.

When you decided to make changes, your vision undoubtedly involved making changes that would have some impact on your and your team's private lives. The decision you made will require some adjustments to your commitment to:

- changing how you do things
- changing how you see things
- changing how you hear things

Making these adjustments will help you to achieve the changes to your business. Somerset Maugham once observed, "If you don't change your beliefs, your life will be like this forever. Is that good news?"

The change planning process requires you to understand your desired outcome. Write down as many things you can think of that need to happen for this outcome to occur. The clearer you are about what must be done, the better the outcome will be.

You should also assess your resources to ensure you have your priorities in balance. Rest, work and reward, food, shelter, and utilities are our foremost priorities in life. Rent a room, rather than a whole office, if a room is all you need. Rest at home as if you were at a resort. Take a break, whether it is going for a drive in the car with a picnic lunch or just looking around and noticing the scenery. Sometimes it may be just the company you keep that improves the activity and your life. You can spend many years of your life doing activities by yourself, even when you are in a relationship. Don't wait to be asked or hope that the relationship will bring those enjoyable and happy events for you. Make it happen for you first, because the purpose of your individual journey is to be happy. According to Edward DeBono, author of *Six Hats,* "Creativity involves breaking out of established patterns in order to look at things in a different way."[41] *Start today.*

There needs to be a certain level of creativity involved when making changes. If you want or need more creativity so you can stay ahead of change in your business, here

---

[41] de Bono, Edward. (1985). *Six Thinking Hats: An Essential Approach to Business Management.* London, England, Little, Brown & Company.

are some techniques, tools, tips, and tactics to consider. Knowing what coloured hat you and your employees are likely to be will stimulate your observations of the members of the project team. Creativity is involved not only in coming up with change ideas but also in actively solving problems, identifying alternatives and options, finding the right people to find solutions, identifying new opportunities, staying ahead of the competition, and maximising returns on your business changes.

To increase creativity, you may also want to consider these reminders:

- Stop making assumptions. Let go of the way it's been done before. Try something different.
- Think differently. Use other people as sounding boards.
- Ask "what if" questions. Who has been your best mentor/idol; what would he or she do with your limited resources.
- Start with the resources instead of the problem. What can you do with them that you're not doing now?
- Get a quantity of ideas and then focus on the best ones. Record all the ideas.
- Take a break to distance yourself from those ideas.
- Use associations, connections, and opposites when reviewing your ideas.

- Think about what you want to achieve. Focus on the solutions. Write down those solutions. Use all the various types of communications available.

Be sure you cater to all the different types of business styles that your team has:

- Is your team likely to be disconcerted by the change? Who will be called upon to implement the action plan you have set up? What type of resistance is likely?
- How are you going to keep things on track?
- How will you ensure that the change is cemented in and becomes the new way of doing things?
- What types of rewards will you use? List these out and stage the delivery.

What problems do you envision occurring with each of the change ideas? Write down the ideas and correlate possible problems for each. What flags are you going to put in place and what will be your response if negative events occur? How will you communicate your response to anything negative? Prepare a schedule of response answers. Always have an answer prepared. How will you recognise a negative event?

When you write your list of change ideas, include how long each is likely to take. How will you establish whether the change has been implemented?

When you focus on the outcome, show consistency and persistence, lead by example, show motivation, provide frequent updates/status of the change, and remind your employees (and yourself) of what the change, if successful, will mean for them.

## Guidelines for the principles of change

Use Table 9 to answer the questions that were raised in the chapter for a specific change you'd like to make. Use the train carriage's concept. Answer the six questions: (1) who is in the first, second or third carriage? (2) What will each of them do? (3) When will they do it? (4) Do they understand why they are doing it? (5) How will they do it—alone or as a group? (6) Where will they do it? Ensure that you have reviewed the behaviours, attitudes, beliefs, and motivations. If you know your employees well, consider listing their names and answering how they are likely to behave and the six "when, where, who, why, how, and what" questions.

Remember that it is your attitude that is the most important one of all. Change yours to where you see adversity as opportunity. Smart leaders communicate, commensurate, commemorate: They act on the results, and communicate early and often what they plan to do. They use excellent customer service to grow trust and confidence, and leverage technology to enhance ongoing communication through electronic newsletters, blogs, webinars, and podcasts.

## Making Changes Easily

| Outcomes you hope to achieve | Why | What | How | Where | Who | When |
|---|---|---|---|---|---|---|
| (1) Move the furniture into an open style plan for your teams | (i) improve communication and visibility for performance | (i) furniture (ii) filing; (iii) phones | Employ furniture movers. | The new design of the office layout will show the new locations for furniture, filing, etc. | (i) facilitation person who will list the action items (ii) boxes for the employees to put their things into before the move | (i) date of the move (ii) time that it will take to move furniture (iii) phone/faxes require supplier support |
| (2) Move the files into a common area with the photocopiers, scanners, and shredders | (ii) centralise all files | (i) layout of the new stationary areas (ii) supplies and orders | (i) quotes for suppliers to top up suppliers (ii) back-up plan for a month order of low items | (i) systemised ordering method (ii) on-line orders for items | Delegated to the admin area for top-ups of supplies | (i) monthly is usually enough; (ii) When there are new projects, anticipate what will have to be ordered. |

Table 9 Outcomes, 5 W's, and How

| Outcomes you hope to achieve | Why | What | How | Where | Who | When |
|---|---|---|---|---|---|---|
|  |  |  |  |  |  |  |
|  |  |  |  |  |  |  |

Also consider preparing a daily action list by using Table 10 to organise your thoughts and activities.

| Top Five Things to Do Today | | |
| --- | --- | --- |
| No. | Item | Outcomes/List |
| 1 | Set meetings for the week ahead by blocking your diary, using either 'booked' or 'tentatively booked' in your diary. | |
| 2 | Set preparation time into the diary so you are ready for meetings. | |
| 3 | Work on one file at a time. Everything else should be put away. When you have finished this file, put it away and start on the next one. | |
| 4 | Take five-minute breaks each hour and move around the office. | |
| 5. | Prepare a list of priorities for the next day before you leave the office so when you leave the office you can focus on your home life. | |
| 6. | | |
| 7. | | |
| 8. | | |

Table 10: Sample Priority List

As Mark Twain once said, "To get the full value of joy you must have someone to divide it with," and with your proposed change plans, there will be many to share with. Make the proposed changes as exciting for your employees as it is for you. When you are happy, then everything around you glows. Remember what Aristotle observed: "Happiness is the meaning and purpose of life, the whole aim and end of human existence."

Feel the abundance and engage in the activities around what you want to change. You are going to make changes in a place where you spend a large portion of your life, so the change must be a positive one, something that makes you get up before the alarm goes off in the morning.

I am twice as happy now about what I am achieving than I have ever been. There were quite a few hard decisions to make when I reviewed my life and priorities, but changes had to be made: I wanted more out of my life, career, and relationships. When I re-evaluated my life, I was able to establish what adjustments and decisions I needed to make and ultimately what had to change in all areas of my life. It was a starting point for change. I asked myself what was great about my life and what more I wanted in my career and relationships, and I noticed a trend. I wasn't being valued by others or myself, as even I put others' needs before my own.

Answering these questions honestly allowed me to create a new beginning that I am now experiencing on a daily basis. The decisions were tough at the time, as some involved people I cared about, but I had to be clear about who and what I wanted in my life going forward—and

## Making Changes Easily

why. Answering those questions and ultimately making those decisions were life-changing experiences. Change takes courage, but it was up to me to bring about my own happiness and success because no one else could give it to me except me.

I reassessed the imposition of other's negative attitudes and poor behaviours on my life. In valuing myself and recognising my life's purpose, changes began to happen. Some people left my life's path and others joined it. My life has changed immensely and, for the most part, for the better. It was a make-over in many ways, and in some cases one of grand proportions. The courage to proceed with those changes has me engaging in activities and being with people that make me excited about life every day. Since I decided to bring about change in my life, I rarely look back to what was. There is a saying that you can't drive a car while looking in the rear view mirror or you will crash into something in front of you. With each day, my life continues to blossom with infinite possibilities having decided to make necessary changes. You too can achieve your own goals and enjoy the outcomes. If you are not being valued in your life's circumstances, then do something about it.

> If you're trying to achieve, there will be roadblocks. I've had them; everybody has had them. But obstacles don't have to stop you. If you run into

a wall, don't turn around and give up. Figure out how to climb it, go through it, or work around it. —Michael Jordon

Always turn a negative situation into a positive situation. —Michael Jordon

# CHAPTER 7

# ESSENTIAL CHANGE MANAGEMENT PRACTICES AND RULES

> All changes, even the most longed for, have their melancholy; for what we leave behind us is a part of ourselves; we must die to one life before we can enter another. —Anatole France

So far you have read advice about how to put your vision into action. You have identified your behaviours, attitudes, beliefs, and motivations and those of your employees. You are contemplating leaving behind so many things that one day you may not remember how it used to be, and that can be a good thing. The principles of change discussed here will help you discover the depth of your employees and what they could contribute through their participation, as well as their possible resistance to change.

The benefits of the brainstorming and workshopping sessions that identified the best ideas are integral to the planning phase. You have a list of ideas that form part of your action plan to implement the business change. Remaining motivated during the change process ensures you have sustainable resources from start to finish. Your commitment coupled with your knowledge of how you and your employees process and put into action the changes will impact all those involved. Your stakeholders play an integral part of the change process and the future of those best ideas.

You don't necessarily need to know every detail pertaining to the principles, practices, and rules of change management, but it will be helpful to understand some of those basics to help you achieve the changes you are proposing to make. Trained specialists can help you work through the technical components, but for now, you have started moving the change train with the brainstorming and workshopping and by understanding the principles of change. Once the change train gains the momentum it needs to reach its destination in the required timeframes with the desired results, you will need to keep up with the changes yourself.

Theorists would have you believe that all your ducks need to be in a row for you to achieve change. I've researched the topic extensively and have experience in several multi-million dollar change projects and have found a few common denominators, but one thing I have discovered through working with teams in project management and change management: You don't have to have all the ducks in a row to get started at all. If you wait for that, you may never get started. When you have employees on board with enthusiasm, preparedness for change, skills, resources and physical and mental energy, then you just do it.

The common features of successful change are:

- getting involvement and achieving engagement
- positioning changes
- planning
- communicating clearly
- listening

Here are more detailed explanations of each of these common denominators.

**Involvement and engagement:** Ensure that everyone is involved and engaged in the process. In large organisations making change is usually best achieved in a layered approach, depending on the type of change.

**Organisational Positioning:** where is the organisation right now? *What* do you want? *When* do you want it? *Why* do you want it? *What* you have to do to get it? *Who* will be affected (stakeholders)?

**Planning:** Ensure that all you have to develop is measurable.

**Communicating clearly:** at the beginning, informative communication will allow for behavioural adaption.

**Listening':** You can't listen when you are talking.

As individuals we all have varying degrees of discipline. In change management, discipline relates to:

- consistency
- delivery in your change programme that highlights the expected challenges
- managing outcomes

Overall it will be consistency that produces the results. Challenging one division to lead by example is a way to ensure everyone is on board with the changes to be made. A valuable case study is the Anglo American approach of using a programme to test the effect and benefits of their asset optimisation process.

Each of the change practices identified is in itself a discipline

**Consistency**: Maintaining momentum through the change phases. Stick to the designed plan, but if it is clear that one aspect of the plan isn't appropriate or is not working, consult with the team again and find a solution.

**Challenge recognition:** Identify what challenges are likely to occur throughout each phase of the change process, and implement a strategy to overcome these challenges. For example, resistance can be addressed through clearer communication and instructions.

**Managing Outcomes:** Ensure that you have a planned reward and recognition process in hand for when things go according to plan. In addition, have a contingency plan for any risk issues that may occur and have a business interruption plan on standby.

**Other considerations:** Recognise the physical/mental energy involved in change management. Change places demands on your and your employees' physical and mental resources. When you are preparing for change, start with the individual(s) who make up your business and its infrastructure. As the owner of the business (or the CEO, CIO, or team leader), ask yourself: Are you ready? Are you really prepared? That is, are you a good leader and clear communicator who is organised, and motivated? It's not necessary to be all of these at once, as your team members and change leader may be able to fill in where you may be lacking, but ensure your team has a good mix of styles in order to be effective. Remember the skills of a good leader that are required to achieve change, such as good communication, the ability to listen, and planning and organising skills.

To keep projects rolling along with sufficient momentum to meet the deliverable timeframes, I usually approach them by *Preparing for the worst, expecting the best, and going with the flow*. Each change project will have its own evolutions, peaks, troughs, eruptions, and disruptions, so you must be as disciplined and consistent as you can too achieve positive results. What are your ground rules for your project?

Some basic ideas for effective change are outlined below: We all need guide rails to ensure that we keep on track and rolling along. The engine driver has the expertise to maintain the engine during the journey. The engine provides the power, and with persistent participation and consistent momentum the train arrives at its destination.

There are several initiatives that you need to consider straight away:

- Employees will do what they perceive is in their own best interest, so if you are going to make changes, they are likely to push back if they don't feel it will be in their best interest to change.
- Humans tend to be uncomfortable with change at the best of times. Some people embrace change readily, but as long as the change has some positive and meaningful outcome/solution for them, most people are eventually receptive.
- People who are uncomfortable with change can become excited and enthusiastic when they are challenged to be creative but will remain uninterested if they are not given an opportunity to play a primary role.
- People differ, so one size does not fit all when it comes to making changes in business.

Your challenge will be giving your employees a taste of what is coming, some idea of the change you are proposing. For example, you can give them the architects/designers' 3D images of the new office space so they can become accustomed to the changes and ease any discomfort or mistrust about what you are proposing to change. When you are looking at long-term changes to the business, where it is more difficult to provide a visualisation of the change, be sure there is clarity in your message. As George Bernard Shaw once said, "The single biggest problem with communication is the illusion that it has taken place," so be sure the message received is the one you meant to send!

The change process starts with setting your vision, which should be simple but strategically driven. Maintaining your motivation and that of your team by keeping the ideas *fresh* in your employees' minds enhances everyone's focus. Communicate clearly and involve as many employees as possible using as many communication tools as possible. Selecting the right project team members requires that you determine that the team has the mix of skills and commitment necessary to achieve the best outcome. If you don't have the right team members, train the employees you have. Empower the change by providing relevant rewards and sufficient recognition for achieving your desired change outcomes. Your strategy as to the phases of change requires adequate layering of each aspect of the programme of change. When the change processes are underdeveloped, disruptions can cause a negative ripple effect across the business. Rather than swamping the team and the organisation with all the changes at once, devise a well-developed plan and a continuous review of the phases to ensure continuity of the plan such that it meets the timeframe for delivery. Understanding and counteracting negativity or resistance to the change can affect the outcome, so keep a watchful eye on the progress to achieve a better outcome overall.

In summary, throughout the change process review your vision and motivation.

- **Vision—do you still have it?** Revisit your vision regularly, and rewarding everyone involved when they achieve milestones. We see, think, and feel change, and our perception of change alters, so each person perceives it differently.
- **Motivation**: Keep as positive as possible throughout the process. Ensure that your team have a balance between their regular responsibilities and those that are part of the project plan.

## Communication

Consistent and positive communication coupled with an effective timeline will provide a clear message about what needs to be done to achieve the goals. As individuals, once

## Making Changes Easily

we accept the concept of change, change is inevitable. Then there's the personal change that occurs when things around us change. Effective communication throughout a project cannot be stressed enough. You or your change manager must provide timely information. As Harold Maslow, developer of Maslow's hierarchy of needs and professor of psychology at Columbia University, said, "If the only tool you have is a hammer, you tend to see every problem as a nail."

The communication mechanism needs to be in language to which everyone can relates, and using the various methods of communication will ensure that the message gets good coverage. To ensure that the information communicated is of high quality, listen for feedback and any concerns from your employees.

What makes a good communication plan? Specify who will receive the change information, when they will receive it,[42] and what type of communication mechanism will be used.[43]

---

[42] A communications plan is a timetable of ongoing delivery of planned communication releases to update all employees. The items in the plan should be varied so the information remains interesting for the receiver.

[43] The types of communication could include broadcasts, video conferencing, newsletters, team meeting notes, and emails that contain updates.

- **The Team**: Put employees with the right skills on your team. They would need to effective in their ability to communicate. How well do you know your project team? Will they all get on together and work well together? Ensure that the team has a good mix of skills and solid commitment to the project. In the event that the team is missing one or the other, you may need to train one or more members. While training can cause delays, the value of the training may be worth the time.
- **Momentum**: Maintain a watchful eye on timeframes, your team, and how your employees are reacting to the change, as all of these can affect the progress of the project. Identify negativity, resistance, or fatigue if the project is a long-term project. Ensure that you are asking questions regularly as to how the individuals are progressing with their action lists. Without ongoing and effective communication the project of change can slow down unexpectedly.

Further planning and implementation, continued communication, and ongoing consultation throughout the project's life will gel the transition and embedding process. The approach to change needs to be planned change rather than reactive change. Planned change is purposeful, designed, and implemented in a timely fashion. Planned change is proactive and includes a vision of all avenues and aspects of the proposed change. Reactive change, on the other hand, tends to be ad hoc and piecemeal with no prior thought.

Processing the plan involves:

- Letting go of the old ways, doing it differently and better. After all, as Edward deBono pointed out, "If you never change your mind, why have one?"
- Action, that is, work involving change, including a transition phase and setting a plan for the new ways.

## Empowerment

Bill Gates described what can happen when workers are empowered when he said,

> Virtually every company will be going out and empowering their workers with a certain set of tools, and the big difference in how much value is received from that will be how much the company steps back and really thinks through their business processes, thinking through how their business can change, how their project management, their customer feedback, their planning cycles can be quite different than they ever were before.

A simple example is when employees are given authority to do something using their own initiative.

One study revealed that employees do not recognise the term "empowerment," nor do they reference the term "power" in relation to themselves. However, they are able to relate to associated concepts, notably "personal responsibility" and "control over their work."[44] As the business owner and possible change leader, you should be aware that empowerment will vary considerably from one person to another. What will you give those that are active participants to help them feel as though they are in charge of the change you are making? Give them opportunities to shine.

**Change Strategy**

The old saying, "if you fail to plan, you plan to fail," is apt here. Use your six serving men to get results:

1. When: fix a date for transition and work backwards.
2. Who: advise your employees of the progress of the plan fortnightly or weekly.

---

[44] Greasley, Kay, Andrew Price, Nicola Naismith, and Robby Soetanto. (1993). *Understanding empowerment from an employee perspective: What does it mean and do they want it?* Loughborough University, Loughborough, UK, Emerald Group Publishing Ltd.

3. What: Describe what is changing, and be specific when delivering the message.
4. Why: Give them a *picture* of your vision and explain why it needs to happen.
5. How: How to implement a change requires thought and planning. The transition can be disconcerting to your employees.
6. Where: Will the change take place in one division or team at a time or in the whole organisation at once?

One of the most important features of effective change management involves effective communication. Communication is often overlooked, and the view that communication should be done only on a "needs to know" basis often gets employees off balance when you most need them to move at the same time and in the same direction. Then there's the verbal sabotage that can take place in an organisation[45]. Letting go of how you used to do things before is often the first big hurdle, and it requires flexibility to overcome. Allow yourself to use fresh eyes to find a new technique to resolve a problem or manage a new situation.

---

[45] Tracy, Brian. (1993). *Maximum Achievement*. New York, USA: Simon and Schuster. This book outlines the importance of improvement and the effects of criticisms.

## Momentum

Momentum is integral to the whole change process and relies on a constant and persistent review of the steps in your change plan. When you review your plan regularly, you will be able keep on track and be able to check off items that have been completed and monitor action items that have deadlines. This kind of ongoing review will help you maintain a nice rhythm in your planned approach to change.

## Vision Outcome

During the process of change, everyone will be undergoing their own changes, whether they are personal changes, business changes, changes to a planning approach, implementation-related changes, consultation-related changes, or communication changes. Your employees will be experiencing some discomfort as a result of any of these types of change. At work, any change can be misinterpreted if it is delivered incorrectly, with resulting mumbling and grumbling to anyone who will listen. Then the "black mould" can start appearing to contaminate a bright idea. By making smaller changes that form part of the larger change, you may be able to generate a momentum that catches on throughout the organisation.

## Time Management

Time is the enemy when it comes to implementing changes and innovative ideas. 'As Malcolm Gladwell pointed out in discussing the concept of the tipping point in his book, *Ready, Fire, Aim*, What separates ideas that cause flood from those that are merely absorbed into the marketplace are... minor variations [on commonly held ideas]. Details matter."[46] There will be a run of change with the masses heading in the new direction—the one you inspired them to follow.

Your change needs to be realistic, achievable, measurable, understandable, manageable, communicable, and consistent. The pace of the change can be slow, moderate, quick, or urgent, depending on your business and the nature of the change. Discuss your strategy with the change leader and the project team.

---

[46] Masterson, Michael. (2008). *Ready, Fire, Aim*. Chichester, Great Britain, John Wiley & Sons.

# Guidelines for change management principles and rules

Think back to your brainstorming session and the workshopping activity you undertook and remind yourself of the following points:

- What were the common features that you and your group came up with?
- What is your business's current position? Are you going to spruce up the business processes so the business can shed some deadwood and expand? What are the answers to the six "why, when, what, who, how, and where" questions?
- How will you communicate the changes to your employees?

Feedback is important to the success of any change project, as is communicating the progress of the change. Always seek good counsel as a way of managing change. People both outside and inside the organisation can give you valuable feedback about the changes proposed. Be on the alert for the saboteurs of the project plan so you can gain their cooperation and help them overcome their fears of the change.

Who will you ask to assist you inside the business who is likely to give genuine feedback on the changes? Who will you ask to assist you outside the business? When communicating about the change, highlight the benefits of the change you are making and provide responses to questions that they may want answered. Keep all of your stakeholders informed.

At the beginning of the change management process, you need to be prepared so you don't go off path in the interim stage of preparing for change. Watch your BACK. The BACK[47] Principle refers to Build, Anticipate, Consider, and Kickback.

**Build** negative responses into the plan so you are prepared.

**Anticipate** what may cause downtime for your change project.

**Consider** the following questions. There will be a lot of other changes going on when you decide to make change in your business. There will be some personal examination underway and if you are alert to some of the types of things that you will be feeling and thinking at this time, then it help you along the way: (1) Where did we learn to think, speak, draw? (2) Why do we think the things that we do? (3) Who has guided you through your life to date? (4) What has/have this/these person(s)

---

[47] The BACK Principle forms part of the time2manage series of seminars conducted by Louise Corica ©2005.

taught you? What was the language used? (5) What are you still hearing in your head? (6) What are those voices telling you still? (7) Why do we keeping thinking this way? (8) If it's negative self-talk, what do we have to do to change this way of thinking? (9) What can you do to think for yourself? (10) What is the difference between a dream and a goal? (Dreams' are in the mind. It is when you decide to do it and set a plan that is capable of materialising that it becomes a goal.)

**Kick back** the questions above in the future sense.

(1) What am I going to learn that will change the way I think, act and do to achieve these outcomes?
(2) What guides will I rely on going forward?
(3) What voice will I listen to now?
(4) What are my dreams now?
(5) What goals do I wish to set for myself?

The principles, practices, and rules of the BACK Principle are a foundation that will support you in developing comprehensive safeguards for your change management plan. Asking powerful questions and answering clearly and concisely will help you and your team to build a basis for a progressive project. You are gaining more insightful information with all of these questions and are moving forward with your vision. Stay focused and positive, and communicate clearly.

# CHAPTER 8

# TECHNIQUES AND TIPS

The team with the best players wins. —Jack Welsh.

We have considered the importance of behaviours, attitudes, beliefs, and motivations when undertaking a project and putting a team together. Once you have brainstormed and workshopped your change idea, written out your five W's plan, and are well into developing the action plans for your visionary ideas of change, you'll need some helpful techniques and tips.

Throughout your change process you'll find it necessary to review, initiate, and create different ways to bring about change, sustain interest, and entrench the new ways of doing things for your business. Now it is time to engage the existing theories so you can maintain progress when making changes in your business.

The de Bono coloured hats[48] are metaphors for each direction in which our brains think, an effective and elaborate segregation of the thinking processes that you

---

[48] de Bono, Edward. (1985). *Six Thinking Hats: An Essential Approach to Business Management*. London, UK Little, Brown & Company.

and your employees may experience during your project of making change. Employment of the concept of the six thinking hats can help you identify issues, problems, and solutions related to ideas, if you apply it prior to selecting your change team participants. In applying this type of identifier concept may assist in selecting the right employees and the right mix of people skills and talents for your project team so you're sure all kinds of thinking are included in the workshopping process.

Can you identify the coloured hat you wear most often?

## Some additional questions to explore:

- Do you make assumptions? If so, stop.
- Can you let go of the old way of doing things? How do you handle trying something different and new?
- Can you think differently? If not, you may need to use other people's skills when sounding out the best ideas for your change implementation.
- Do you ask "what if" questions to find solutions to the problems you have? Who have been your best mentors/idols? What would they do with your limited resources? Your own reading and research may find a lot of options and alternatives that will work for you.
- Can you entertain a quantity of ideas without judging and then choose the highest quality ideas?

- Do you record all the ideas submitted and consider using mind-mapping techniques?
- Do you take a break from time to time to distance yourself from those ideas?
- When you hit a roadblock or the ideas dry up and you can't find an answer, do you use your associates and connections to support you? Sometimes a different perspective or an opposing idea can make a significant difference.
- Do you think about what you want to achieve and write it down? Do you use all the different types of communications to cater to all the different types of business styles that are in your company?
- What types of discomfort are you likely to experience? What and who will be called to enact the plan? What type of resistance is likely?
- How are you going to keep things on track?
- How will you ensure that the change is cemented into your business and becomes the new way of doing things?
- What types of rewards will you give to reinforce the achievements? List those out and stage the delivery.

When planning a change, there are five phases for you to work through:

1. Letting go
2. Discomfort

3. Taking action
4. Transition
5. Setting the change

**Phase 1: Letting go:** This first and most important phase is a time to reformulate new ways to introduce new ideas. You arrived at this point because of how you were thinking, so you must first change your thinking. You may have been hearing employees' ideas and comments, which may not have been what you wanted to hear. A change is going to happen, but whether it is positive or negative is up to you.

**Phase 2: Discomfort:** There will be discomfort with the shift from where you were to where you are going. It may be a radical change if you need to change the culture of your business. If you haven't thought about cultural change, remember that change requires the ability to review, revive, and renovate! As you would address the need to update your home, your business may need refurbishment. If a change is perceived as a negative, that negativity can be like a mould that spreads throughout the business environment. The whispers of discontent will grow and take over whatever they touch, so work to sustain a positive outlook from the beginning of the change project to the end to ensure that you and your team members don't run out of enthusiasm and momentum. A positive outlook also keep you open to review and re-evaluation, as some changes require that your resources be rerouted and your approach to the change programme be renewed—sometimes at the same time.

**Phase 3: Taking action:** A central feature of change is the "doing." To ensure that everyone gets to the desired end state, break down each component of the change, know what is involved, and share the process with your employees. The element of speed is also a vital consideration, as many innovative changes require speed while others require gradual implementation. Transforming your business one person and one division at a time requires a level of creativity. Combining the right level of speed with innovative techniques will culminate in positive outcomes and positive results.

**Phase 4: Transition:** Expect discomfort, and keep going. Discuss the issues, work through the issues, find solutions, and aim for a win-win outcome. Expect resistance, but talk through it using effective and clear communication. Expect the unexpected, and talk more, and listen more. At this stage of making change some level of anxiety about the loss of effectiveness and self-esteem in relation to the work is natural. Anxiety is the primary cause of defensive reactions to change, but your real work lies in getting people to let go of the old ways, to release anything that you and your employees are holding onto that threatens the effectiveness of the change you are proposing. Helping them overcome these uncertainties will improve the next phase.

What resistance can you think of that is likely to occur in each phase? What do you need to anticipate right now? (1) employees who are uninformed and misperceive the information you have provided about the change, (2) resource requirements, (3) the need for new technology, and (4) the need for training to achieve the changes. Your employees may not see your vision, the big picture, or the outcome, so keep communicating to help your employees overcome these uncertainties.

**Phase 5: Setting the Change:** This phase sets the change in place and becomes the new foundation for growth and a platform for expansion and new beginnings. The change must be consistent with your company's core values, or employees will have difficulty accepting and adopting the changes, let alone the new guidelines and procedures in the business.

So how are you feeling so far about driving the new change to your business?

- Have you provided the facts and relevant data to connect the change effort to the present way your company is doing things?
- What image have your painted for what you want the company to look like and what will happen if

things don't change to motivate your employees to your way of thinking or allow them to adopt the idea as their own?

- Have you involved your employees in the most effective way? When you provide the facts, expect a reaction—both positive and negative. Remember that you are asking them to make changes that will affect them in some way.
- Have you created small, achievable goals?
- Have you created momentum?
  - Have you provided coaching and mentoring, or do you have someone available to provide guidance?
  - Are you creating change through celebrations regularly, depending on the features of your change project?
  - Are you embedding the change by using a semi-formal process that will later become the formal systems and structure?
  - Are you giving notice of change using innovative and interesting techniques? The longer it takes to implement the change, the more creative the communications should be. Keep it interesting. For example, you can use a media alert, a YouTube video, or an internal memo about the change.

## Rewards and Recognition

We all like to receive some type of reward and recognition at some point in our lives for what we are doing or have achieved.

Stephen Covey, author of *The 7 Habits of Highly Effective People*,[49] said, "An empowered organization is one in which individuals have the knowledge, skill, desire, and opportunity to personally succeed in a way that leads to collective organisational success." Ensure that your plan has regular rewards, which can be as simple as a movie pass. Put the reward infrastructure into the change process, and discuss the most motivating types of rewards among the change team, considering all participants. You may want to consider a financial remuneration for a completed project, but also consider milestone rewards, such as a special lunch, as small celebrations boost morale and acknowledge contributions. Performance management is the process of rewarding employees for the good things they do and challenging them to continue to work hard.

Change doesn't have to be difficult, but for any transformation in your business to be successful, more than just the structure and operations of your business

---

[49] Covey, Stephen. (1999). *The 7 Habits of Highly Effective People*. New York, USA: Simon and Schuster.

must change. In *The Heart of Change*,[50] Kotter and Cohen explained that people think and feel differently, so keep this in mind when you are asking them to share their comments on your change vision. When you connect with employees and their emotions, you will observe changes in their behaviour that will either support or obstruct your plan for change. Kotter and Cohen argued that "change initiatives often fail because leaders rely too exclusively on data and analysis to get buy-in from their teams instead of creatively showing or doing something that appeals to their emotions and inspires them to spring into action."[51]

When you are going to bring about change, there are ten features to include:

1. Motivation: Keep yourself and your employees motivated by keep things *fresh* and ready for change.
2. Leadership: Ensure that you are the right fit for the role, or select an independent facilitator for change.

---

[50] Kotter, John P., and Dan S. Cohen. (2012). *The Heart of Change: Real-Life Stories of How People Change Their Organizations.* Boston, Massachusetts, USA Harvard Business Review Press.

[51] Kotter, John P., and Dan S. Cohen. (2012). *The Heart of Change: Real-Life Stories of How People Change Their Organizations.* Boston, Massachusetts USA: Harvard Business Review Press.

3. Team members: Team members need to blend together and have the right mix of skills and commitment to achieving the change.
4. Vision: The vision should be simple and strategic and driven correctly and efficiently.
5. Communication: Involve as many employees as possible, and use technology.
6. Empowerment: Ensure that there is reward/recognition for achieving desired outcomes.
7. Phases of the change strategy: Layer the processes rather than swamping the team and the organization.
8. Modifications and reassessments of the change strategy: Revisit proposed changes to ensure the best result.
9. Momentum/Continuity—Ensure that the phases are strategically set and that they have flow and momentum.
10. End result: Ensure that the outcome is reinforced and that you identify the benefits of the change you are introducing.

While there are a number of academic approaches to establishing the business style of the employees on your change team, Edward DeBono's "six hats" can be helpful in giving you another perspective of the changes you envisage for your business. The techniques and tips of the six hats will enhance your ability to recognise your team members' styles in order to bring about change. The importance of reward and recognition should not be overlooked when achieving milestones in the project.

Table 11 will give you a basis for insights into your team's strengths.

| Hat Type | Strengths that you demonstrate | Which team members have this strength |
|---|---|---|
| Hat #1 (white)—information, facts | | |
| Hat #2 (red)—emotions, intuition, gut reactions | | |
| Hat #3 (black)—discernment, caution, conservativeness | | |
| Hat #4 (yellow)—optimism, benefits, harmony | | |
| Hat #5 (green)—creativity | | |
| Hat #6 (blue)—meta thinking | | |

Table 11: The Six Hats Types for Change Processes

## CHAPTER 9

# CHANGE AND PRODUCTIVITY

When you bring about change, there is always a chance that productivity in your business will be affected and activities will slow down. Freeman, author of *Labour Productivity Indicators*, observed, "Labour productivity is a revealing indicator… as it offers a dynamic measure of growth, competitiveness, and living standards within an economy."[52] During change implementation you will be asking existing employees to undertake work that is not part of their usual daily activities. So you may need to make some concessions. Productivity levels may begin to change too, so expectations that you will meet some production quotas may need to be revised.

When you are visualising what the *new look* your business will have, are you seeing:

- the vision of what you want your business to look like? What you want to achieve should be at the forefront of your mind.

---

[52] Freeman, R. (2008). *Labour productivity indicators.*, University of Chicago Press, Chicago, and (2010) by the National Bureau of Economic Research printed in USA.

- everything that needs to change for your business during the change process? Your stakeholders—your suppliers, service providers and shareholders—should have a high priority, as your change can affect your products, services, and brand.
- well-developed quarterly, half-yearly, and annual business plans, as well as annual strategic-planning days, prepared and delivered that include what you are proposing to develop? Your business plans and strategic plans must be aligned. Undertaking activities that are incongruous with your overall plan will be detrimental to the outcome of your change plans. Once you have a clear plan and strategy for your business, review it frequently. Most larger organisations cannot function effectively without close examination of such documents.
- yourself, as well as the business, fit and healthy? Your mental and physical health should be your top priority. Your business fitness often mirrors your own.
- possible compromising situations that can affect you and your business unnecessarily because you are not proactive on all challenges? Do you know what challenges your business faces?
- sustainable enthusiasm when undertaking business discussions? It is easy to start off being

excited and energetic, but these feelings can dissipate quickly and lead to fatigue. Maintain your business's "fitness" during your change project.

There are several leadership skills at which you should excel when you have decided to bring about change in your business. Keep these seven leadership skills at the forefront of your strategy:

(1) **Problem recognition** involves noticing when the proposed changes are not working. It's like noticing oil on the garage floor. Was it really the first sign, that there was a problem with your vehicle? Did you notice any noises before that, or did you wait until smoke was coming out of the car exhaust? How long did it take before you decided to do something about it?

(2) **Responsibility** involves acknowledging that there is an issue with some part of the process, communicating it appropriately, and following up until it's resolved. Some employees are keen to take responsibility if something isn't going to plan, but the first responsibility rests with you and the change manager.

(3) **Communication** through effective dialogue and a desire to work things out can help you anticipate problems. Progress reporting is always a great approach, as the use of updates can

reveal weaknesses when employees mention it in meetings. Ask questions, ask again, and keep asking. A golden rule of communication is that there are three sides to a controversy: yours, the other person's, and the right one.

(4) **Persistence** is required to keep working the changes and to ask questions so you can see things from everyone's point of view.

(5) **Broad-mindedness** involves working at being open to course corrections and to other people's ideas and solutions. Being firm is different from being stubborn or being stuck.

(6) **Being Practical** and realistic means keeping the approach to making change as simple as possible, as solutions work better when they are simple. Manage the change through consistent adjustments throughout the project, and keep the programme of change flexible for all the participants so your employees can keep up with the change as it goes along. If you need new equipment, give your employees training on it so you can roll out the new technology as part of the project timetable.

(7) **Optimism** makes you the shining example of positivity throughout the change project. Even though you may want to assume the foetal position when things don't go according to plan, use your physical and mental strength to stay on

track. You can also ask for help, as you have a network of employees who are waiting for you to ask.

I have discovered from my own experience the value of energy in projects. To give you an idea of how much energy you will need to work through each phase, the letting-go phase and the taking-action phase each take about 30 percent of the effort, while the transition and setting the change phases each take about 20 percent. The percentages reflect the level of resistance to change that you are likely to encounter in each phase, and the amount of effort the change is likely to require.

Change management is like spring cleaning. Cleaning the features of your business that are not effective or efficient any longer requires improving business efficiencies. As part of change consider de-cluttering your personal space and refreshing your outlook on what needs to change. Review aspects of your business that can be changed continuously.

How big a broom do you need for the job? Consider these tips: First, discard any ideas that you are not proposing to use right away. They can be reintroduced later, if necessary, when the time is right. Second, establish and build the self-esteem of your team. Third, ensure that the business plan is dusted off and re-checked quarterly. You are challenging yourself and your employees, and all are being called to action as your vision becomes a reality and your purpose and participation are redefined.

When discussing change with your change project team, keep in mind the power of effective communication, which must include:

- the hard facts
- a clear picture of the changes to be made
- the extent of their involvement
- phases of the project in small, manageable pieces
- continuous reporting of the change outcomes
- the training required
- motivational activities and encouragement
- wins and rewards
- creativity

Letting go of "how you did things before" is a challenge that can be difficult for many people. With change, we are required to do things differently and act differently, and we hope that the outcome will be beneficial for us. Although some businesspeople can make a quick decision to let go of an idea if it's detrimental or irrelevant, most of us must take time to "unlearn" what we have been taught or learned from experience. Change requires a different mindset and involving other minds in the change process to ensure a better outcome overall.

If an approach is not working, ask people for their views.

> We have had drilled into us that we need approval of others, We are "obedient" to "please someone", or similar commentary and so on. So don't allow confusion to distort what you are hoping to achieve. You will find a way through the maze if you are experiencing confusion at different times throughout the change process. The behaviour of "changing our minds quickly" is often more apparent in our adult years... A genuine friendship in personal or business life can be a tangible commodity, however requires mutual support.[53]

Trump and Zanker commented that "Too many people think too much about their current situation, instead of thinking about what could be."[54] Spending too much time on a problem can be detrimental, so stop, review, reassess, regain your focus, and create a new way of achieving your goals. You may need to be tougher about making change than you think. As Trump and Zanker pointed out, "Don't get caught up in all the crap. Acknowledge

---

[53] Chin-Ning Chu. (1992). "Thick Face, Black Heart." In *Preparation of Unlearning*. Sydney Australia: Allen & Unwin.

[54] Trump, Donald, and Bill Zanker. (2008). *Think Big, Kick Ass in Business and Life*. New York: Harper Collins.

## Making Changes Easily

the problem and then shift your attention immediately to possible solutions."[55]

Your vision for change may simply be a spring cleaning of your business processes and procedures. The use of a due diligence may highlight some significant resource issues, but they can be overcome by planning and setting goals in line with proposed changes. A different viewpoint will provide a different solution.

Have fun making changes and with all the activities along the way, and be sure to reward yourself. It can be pleasurable to declutter, dump things that don't work for you anymore, refresh, revive, and generally clean up your business activities. There is more to productivity than achieving results, so ensure that the journey is as comfortable as possible for all involved while gaining traction for the new vision.

In addition to all the positive "do" approaches to making change in your business, be aware of five important "don't says." Listen closely for them, and be sure you are not the one saying them. Don't say:

- "We tried that before."
- "That won't work."

---

[55] Trump, Donald, and Bill Zanker. (2008). *Think Big, Kick Ass in Business and Life.* New York, Harper Collins.

- "But"
- "Here's how it will turn out."
- "We've always done it this way."
- "If it ain't broke, don't fix it."

Negativity is a bad habit and has no place in the change challenge. When negativity flourishes, nothing else does. These phrases will affect your team's motivation and creativity when you are having discussions, brainstorming, and think tanks. Keep positive and stay focused.

## Change and its impact on productivity

What problems do you envision with each of your change ideas? Write down the ideas and correlate the problems to each. What indicators or alarms will you set in place, and what will your responses to those alarms be if they occur? How will you communicate the response? Always have an answer or a solution prepared. Then write down how long each change on your list of changes will take. How will you establish whether the change is received positively?

**Tip:** Focus on the outcome by: (a) demonstrating persistence and leading by example, (b) showing your continued motivation to implement the changes, (c) continually providing updates/status of the changes, and (d) reminding your employees of what the change will

## Making Changes Easily

mean for them and the business. Most changes will cause changes in productivity, as your employees are required to do their normal work along with the change plan. The reduction in productivity may also be a result of fatigue from increased workloads. Anticipate these issues and provide support or other incentives when they reach project milestones.

# CHAPTER 10

# PUTTING IT ALL TOGETHER

> Never be afraid to do something new. Remember: amateurs built the ark, professionals built the *Titanic*. —Richard J. Needham

By now you should feel like you can achieve just about anything. At this point in your preparation, review the due diligence that you performed following the workshopping. In reviewing the due diligence information, ask yourself whether:

(a) everyone understands the change idea and concepts, and the outcome you are aiming for
(b) your approach to change is going to be effective because your message is clear
(c) the required project approach and procedures are in place before, during, and after the change process
(d) you have a list of the methods to be used to bring about the changes you are proposing
(e) you have a list of the systems required for the changes
(f) you have reviewed the ideas that will work and those that are not likely to apply just yet

With change comes responsibility. The business owner, the executive, and the change manager, not the employees, are fully responsible for the change. The employees will form part of the team working through the changes, but it is up to the change manager and you to ensure that the facilitation is effective so change can occur. It is up to the executive/owner to interpret, communicate, and enable change, not to impose or instruct it.

Consider using surveys as part of your due diligence, as they can uncover information that will not otherwise be apparent. The responses you received can help you overcome mistrust of the proposed changes and repair misperceptions or misunderstandings before they can cause damage.

The following questions can help you through the last phase before you make your changes:

(a) What are the phases of the change strategy you have in mind? Have you layered the process? Rather than swamping the participants and teams, ensure there are sufficient breaks throughout the change process, especially if it is going to take more than a few months. What will they be, when will they occur? How will you communicate the breaks?

(b) Has momentum for the change process been strategically applied? Going with the flow to sustain the momentum may work, but utilise other approaches when the change process slows.
(c) What positive attitudes are going to use to reinforce the outcomes and benefits of the change?
(d) What attitudes are you looking for and which attitudes will be trying to adjust?

Smart leaders communicate and reward their people for a job well done. Don't just sit in your office sending out emails. Be proactive: walk around, engage in conversations with your employees personally, and coach your managers to do the same. Talk to your employees about what is going on and *listen* to what they have to say.

One way to be effective is to communicate early and often what you plan will be. The plan should include customers, suppliers, third-party providers, and shareholders. Change will apply to some if not all employees however it will depend on what change you are proposing to bring about. Leverage technology to enhance the communication method and consider electronic newsletters, blogs, Facebook, Twitter, and so on and communicate meaningfully.

Employees generally are not keen about learning that you ate veal parmigiana for dinner on Sunday, so make sure your business webinars and podcast updates all contribute to meeting the needs of your audience. Keep it interesting, and tailor it to your audience.

Take stock of where you are in the overall change process. By being realistic and considering the principles, practices, techniques, tips, and some required adjustments along the way, you will progress through the many challenges of change. In setting change goals for your business, you may stretch yourself like never before.

You may have learned a great deal from answering the questions posed so far and reviewing the results from the assessments and due diligence. You can make progress on the changes you have envisioned, from when you first come up with the idea until you have achieved the ideal outcome.

How do you assess your progress now? You can determine your level of success by: (a) looking at the list of problems you have identified and found solutions for and how you have grown from the experience, (b) whether you have worked through your plan, maintaining an even keel throughout the journey, (c) how wisely you have used resources, and (d) whether you have developed a secure environment for your employees during this change process.

Remember the three operational concepts that you have brought with you to this point: (a) your commitment to your goals, (b) your constant awareness and observations on the changing conditions around you, and (c) your preparedness to make change happen in consultation with your change team and employees.

When you assess your situation, look carefully at where you are now, where you hope to end up, and what you actually achieve at the conclusion of your change process. Is your plan on schedule?

Did you do enough research on your change approach? What work is required to ensure that your people will be able to adapt to the changes you are proposing?

Did you negotiate aspects of the changes you wanted to achieve? This approach will place you in a better position when making changes across the business.

How about the timing? While this topic has been raised before, it is an essential component to the delivery of the change process you are proposing.

The pace you need to maintain throughout the change programme is strategic because, if you throw all of your energy into one phase, there won't be much energy left for you to carry out the other phases.

The previous chapters have provided recommendations and suggestions as to how to approach change based on understanding the principles, practices, and rules of change, along with the need for engagement. Change projects are not without conflict, and it is often difficult to introduce in the workplace, as employees usually become comfortable with the way things are. What you say and how you say it can have a major impact on how your employees handle the change and whether they avoid it or present conflicting positioning, scepticism, or negativity.

## Counteracting negativity

Expect that your employees will ask a lot of questions about what you are proposing to change and that they will not all like all of what is proposed. However, you have embarked on the change for a good reason and that can overcome questions like "What's in it for me?" and "Will it affect my status in the company?"

The Kubler-Ross Grief Model[56] addresses the emotional issues associated with change effectively. While there are four emotional states experienced during the change process, we examine only the first two, denial and resistance, for the purposes of understanding what you can expect in implementing a business change: If you

---

[56] Kubler-Ross, Elizabeth. (1969). *On Death & Dying*. New York: Simon and Schuster/Touchstone.

hear someone use one of the five "don'ts" mentioned in Chapter Nine, address the issue with the person in order to neutralise the negativity. When you understand the denial and resistance your employees may feel during change projects, you can counteract these emotions with answers that can help overcome them.

Denial usually comes with comments like "I can't believe this is happening to me" and "Why are they doing this?" Questions or fears about the change initiative will need to be answered quickly, often with repetition of messages offered in communication of the message of change. As part of your preparation for change, answer such questions in a newsletter or in your presentation on change.

Resistance to a change process is common. Employees may attempt to slow down or derail the change initiative through negative whispers to try to derail the changes. Sometimes the workplace is like a big school with big kids and big egos. If you anticipate resistance and then recognise where it is coming from, you can overcome it with effective planning and strategies. Resistance is a reaction to change characterised by noisy responses and lack of interest.

Asking for feedback from these employees lets you know quickly where they stand and what they like and dislike so you can approach your change goals and objectives

## Making Changes Easily

effectively. Kubler-Ross describes this emotional state: "Throughout life, we get clues that remind us of the direction we are supposed to be headed... If you stay focused, then you learn your lessons."[57]

Napoleon Hill, author of *Think and Grow Rich*, observed that "Whatever the mind of man can conceive and believe it can achieve."[58] An excellent example of this point of view is Edwin Barnes, who thought his way into partnership with Thomas Edison.[59] Barnes wanted to be in business with Edison, and his journey to meet with and finally discuss his ambitious dream with Edison took all of his desire, focus, and belief. Your thoughts during this change process can create the same type of miracle for you. During the change process remind yourself that, if something doesn't feel right, then it's not right for you. It is important to manage the progress of change throughout the duration of the change.

As you make further changes and reset your goals, first visualise what you want your business to look like at the end of the change process. Once you have that

---

[57] Kubler-Ross, Elizabeth. (1969). *On Death & Dying*. New York: Simon and Schuster/Touchstone.

[58] Hill, Napoleon. (1960). *Think and Grow Rich*. Oxford, Great Britain, Ballentine Books.

[59] Hill, Napoleon. (1960). *Think and Grow Rich*. Oxford, Great Britain, Ballentine Books.

image entrenched in your mind, ask yourself what your approach will do for you. Revisit the reporting process if the change is to take place over an extended period of time. Develop quarterly and half yearly plans, and ensure that you and your employees are keeping physically and mentally fit and healthy during the process.

## Keeping fit during the change process

You could compromise your business if you don't ensure you keep fit. We often start off enthusiastically when we have a great idea. Then, when fatigue sets in when we hit obstacles and get overwhelmed with what has to be done, all of our good intentions and enthusiasm can fade away and compromise the process. (That's why gyms make you pay for your membership up front.)

### *Tips*

- Dump ideas that don't work.
- Try something new every month.
- Work on sustaining your self-esteem and those of your employees.
- Give your business plan the occasional shake-up. Check it monthly, then quarterly, then every six months, and then annually if the change project will take that long. Add the change and then act

## Making Changes Easily

on it. Keep your eye on trends associated with what you want to change.
- Review the plan to ensure that it fits your strategy.
- Change whatever it is that needs changing from your first formulation.
- Maintain your effort and energy in order to be effective.

Negative comments, attitudes, and behaviours are usually just bad habits. When negative comments are allowed to flourish, nothing else does, so creativity grinds to a halt. Staying positive and keeping focused on the end result requires sustained energy and discipline.

Therefore, move promptly and strategically when making a change in your business, as change doesn't like indecision. There can be no more excuses. Use workshopping to work through difficult issues related to the change, and establish a performance-improvement plan for the change process to help sustain interest.

From the beginning, sustain your own motivation as well as that of your participants by keeping things interesting. Freshness keeps minds alert, positive, and focused on the change process. Keep the change concepts in the forefront of the minds of all who are involved in the change management programme.

## Leading Change Successfully

Team members must have the right mix of skills and a firm commitment to achieve the desired outcome of change. If you have a small family business, you may need an experienced consultant, a business associate, or a business friend to meet with from time to time to discuss ideas. Such mentors can help you keep up with what's new in your field. Medium to large organisations will often have this skill base in house, but if not, consider bringing someone in.

Successful change requires a considerable amount of detail in the planning, and sufficient time to:

- select the team
- re-evaluate and stress-test the clarity of your vision of change
- commit consistently and constantly when communicating the message of change
- bring about the changes you envision
- use all your team's behaviours and skills to benefit the process
- revitalise any negative attitudes among your participants with more information

**Selecting the team:** Ensure that you know your employees and use the ones with the right commitment, skills, and level of participation.

**Getting the vision right:** Start with a simple vision, a simple concept, a simple strategy, a 1 × Idea, 1 × action plan. Focus on the creativity of that vision, the outcome, the drivers that will keep the vision going, the efficiencies, and the best results. Implement the change in small portions or phases. Especially when the plan is large, phasing in is beneficial for all involved.

**Communication:** Consider the types of communications that are at play in our day-to-day living, and at work: verbal, non-verbal, and written. Is an email the best way to communicate a particular message? Would a chat on the phone or in person be more or less effective?

**Making change happen:** How you approach the topic of change depends on your leadership style and skills. (I know that this may come as a surprise to a few readers, but some of the best public examples of leadership are politicians.) If you are going to lead a change, determine whether you are an encouraging articulate leader, a relationship specialist, or a mediocre presenter with experience? Are you prepared to be aligned with the employees you will work with on these change ideas? How well do you know them? How easily do *you* adapt to change and changing situations? Michael Roberto wrote, "Fundamentally, leadership is about transforming people in an organisation and leading them to higher performance as a result."[60]

**Recruiting the best project participants with the right skills:** When there is innovative change, everyone involved needs to understand the desired outcome of your change idea. When your employees or stakeholders have misperceptions about the proposed change, counteract those misperceptions with the answers to possible questions that they may have.

**Revitalise where there is negativity:** Staying ahead of change and negativity requires creativity. Having the answers to the questions employees may have will always counterbalance the negativity and whispers that attempt to derail your change ideas. Most change process leaders require the ability to:

- solve problems using problem-solving techniques
- generate more ideas as time goes by
- find options and solutions for change
- identify opportunities
- stay ahead of the competition to maximise business returns

---

[60] Roberto, Michael A. (2011). *Transformational Leadership: How Leaders Change Teams, Companies and Organisations.* Virginia: The Teaching Company.

## Making Changes Easily

Write down what you are going to say when you present your ideas. Here are some reminders for you to work with:

- Stop making assumptions. Try it; it may work this time, and if it doesn't, try something else, such as a variation of what was proposed. You have a team to support you. Ask.
- Think differently. Use different minds to find a better outcome.
- Ask "what if" questions.
- Seek a quantity of ideas and then find the high-quality ones.
- Allow no judgments from those contributing to the pool of ideas.
- Record all the ideas submitted by using mind-mapping.
- Take a break, and distance yourself from the ideas before you undertake a detailed review and prepare a due diligence report.
- Use all the possible associations, connections and opposites when you are looking for new ideas.
- Think about what you want to achieve.

There is no one method that will resolve all of your problems, but be sure-footed and prepared to make changes mid-stream if it's necessary in order to make progress. Combine innovative ideas and elements of change, and provide some flexibility in the planning to account for interruptions and lack of focus on the end goal. By making slight changes regularly, you may achieve far greater results than you would with a less well-planned change process.

## Recovery: when something doesn't go according to plan

Staying ahead of change requires a certain level of creativity, especially when it comes to problem-solving techniques, generating new or varied ideas, finding solutions, identifying opportunities, and staying ahead of the competition.

What do you do when something doesn't go to plan? Here are some tips to help you cope:

- Don't panic. You need a clear head.
- Recheck the proposed delivery of the idea.
- Recheck all the steps taken to this point. Recheck the skills required to carry it through. Do you have enough? If you have the requisite skills on your team, but there is no apparent change, ask your employees why.
- Change your approach. Review the outcome. When you have reached a point where it is difficult to progress, remember what Einstein said: "You can't solve problems by using the same kind of thinking we used when we created them." That

## Making Changes Easily

is why it is important to bring in other people when something doesn't go to plan—so you can use different minds to solve the problem(s).

The reason your participants can't achieve your desired outcome may not be obvious to you. Are they suffering from boredom, stress, or apathy? Often we are not as equipped with the necessary skills as we may first think, and sometimes the best-laid plans can go awry if we are weak in some required skill. Taking on a specialist can make the difference. Remember that you must:

- Know yourself: As the team leader or a strategic part of the change process, know your capabilities, strengths, and weaknesses.
- Be flexible: Remain open to new ideas in times of change. Are you prepared to take an alternate course if it's a better one, or are you likely to dig in your heels and not budge?
- Maintain a positive attitude: Attitudes go up and down during times of change, often because of fluctuating energy levels. Ensure that your attitude remains positive and inspiring as much as possible. In *Maximum Achievement*, Brian Tracy reminded us that, "If you think you can or think you can't, you're right."[61]

---

[61] Tracy, Brian. (1993). *Maximum Achievement*. New York, USA: Simon and Schuster.

With change there are usually upsets and conflicts, and not everyone shares the vision initially or even throughout the entire project, but they go along with it anyway. We all have a variety of experiences that have changed us, but we should not allow them to impair our view of an opportunity when it is the right time for something new to happen. Just because something didn't work last time doesn't mean it isn't going to work now. Consider reviewing why it didn't work to identify what needs to change this time around.

## How thinking processes affect us

We all have different business styles, we all think and act differently, and each of us has a wealth of life and business experiences to draw on when making decisions. More importantly, we need to be mature enough to let go of old ideas and seek new ways to achieve desirable results. Self-esteem, self-awareness, and the power of positive thinking are important components of successful outcomes. Brian Tracy said that you "need courage to be your own psychotherapist. You require tremendous honesty."[62] Therefore, you must be willing to look within yourself to be able to make necessary corrections to yourself or to a change management process. How

---

[62] Tracy, Brian. (1993). *Maximum Achievement*. New York, USA: Simon and Schuster, 234.

## Making Changes Easily

will you respond to making the changes you propose? Remember Brian Tracy's advice that "Stress is not contained in external events, there is no such thing as an inherently stressful situation. There are only stressful responses."[63]

Above all, stay focused on what it is you want to achieve. Aim to be innovative, and integrate your ideas to revolutionise your business. Be observant to your reactions during the change process and consider whether you need to change your inner self-talk, your priorities, your motivation, your habits, your friends, your level of commitment, how you do things, your methods, your routine, and how you think about and spend your money. Some of these changes may warrant only light adjustments, whereas others may require major adjustments. Let's take a closer look at each of these ten common considerations in turn.

**Changing inner self-talk:** Review what you are telling yourself. Listen closely to what you hear yourself saying when you are deliberating over what you want to change. Still your mind when you notice negative commentary starting to creep in and revert to the positive conversations your inner voice will deliver. Prepare some positive comments for when you notice yourself becoming negative. One I use is "I really can do this."

---

[63] Tracy, Brian. (1993). *Maximum Achievement*. New York, USA: Simon and Schuster, 235.

**Changing your priorities:** Nothing changes if nothing changes. *Review your work priorities.* If you don't change your approach to your workload, you are less likely to see significant changes.

**Changing your motivation:** You need to stay positive in the vision of what you hope to achieve and in the development and planning phases of change, as this will help you keep motivated to accomplish your goal of change. You may have experienced this at a time when you decided you needed to go to the gym or cut back on that extra piece of pie.

**Changing your habits:** Old habits die hard! We naturally have an affinity for doing things the same way we have been doing them, as those ways are easy and proven. However, habits can be psychological stumbling blocks for many people as we become too comfortable in what we do and how we do it, even when it's not efficient, productive, or necessary. We put our socks on right foot first, then the left. We have a preferred colour. We go to work the same way every day. We go to the same shopping centre and department store. Why? So we don't have to think about it. Look closely at the way you do these simple tasks and consciously over the next week do the opposite or do it all differently. Monitor how you feel when you do things differently. At first, it's harder; it requires more thought, and we want to go back to the old way. However, the change can also generate new ideas, innovative opportunities, and a refreshed way of seeing things—a change of scenery that you needed.

**Changing your friends:** I don't mean that you should dump the friends you have, but look at who surrounds you and whether you and they create positive synergies. Do they support you and your ideas? Do they simply agree with you and never challenge you? Are they likely to talk you out of doing something because it doesn't suit what they know, understand, or want? Do they help you think things through when you have a new idea? While you shouldn't need someone else to validate you and your ideas, we all need support. Are they likely to laugh at your idea or consider it audacious? Consider taking yourself out of your own comfort zone, and move in different circles. Sometimes we become comfortable being with people who agree with us all the time, but we never grow or experience challenges in this way, so take yourself out of your own comfort zone.

**Changing your level of commitment:** Change your level of commitment to the change. We are starting fresh here, and there are new opportunities and successes to be had. You may be out of your comfort zone doing what you are proposing to do, but go for it anyway. Are you a leader, a follower, or a complacent bystander? Remember your commitment to change and reaffirm it.

**Changing how you do things:** Your routine is just that: routine. Changing how you do things can make your day more productive. For example, rise an hour earlier to exercise before work instead of waiting until evening, when you are tired. When a company I worked for changed its office lease to another location, it was exciting because it reduced my travel time and gave me more time for myself and some personal goals. Instead of driving to work, I went by train. Consequently, I reduced my commute time in traffic and didn't have to wait to arrive home to do my reading and study. Instead of driving, I chose to change how I approached my travel plans and activities each day and ultimately achieved some personal goals. By making such changes, you too can gain time for your personal goals.

**Changing your methods:** Technology can also make you more productive. The Wi-Fi in the train carriages means that you can use a laptop, a tablet, or a smartphone when you travel. Focus on what you are interested in or prepare for work so you can focus on home when you are home. Ensure that you have at least one hour at the beginning of the day at the office when you are not interrupted by employees, phones, or emails. Before you leave in the evening, allow at least ten minutes to prepare your timetable and task list for the next day so you can focus on your top five priorities When you are at home, do what you need to do for your home and family. Be present. Make a similar priority list for what you need to do at home, including spending quality time with one of the kids or your spouse. The simplicity of the approach allows you to focus on the present and avoid spending time on low-priority tasks or having your mind at work when you're at home or your mind at home when you're at work.

**Changing your direction:** A sailor needs to change course by only one degree to end up at quite a different destination than planned when he or she started out. Make course corrections when the project of change is underway so you don't end up where you didn't intend to be.

**Changing your routine:** Making changes to the sequence of events—that is, the time of day that you do things—can put your day in a new perspective. If your productivity needs improvement, consider closing your office door for one hour or not allowing any interruptions if you work in an open area. Always negotiate the time you need to finish the part of your work that needs your undivided attention.

## Summary

> The idea flow from the human spirit is absolutely unlimited. All you have to do is tap into that well. It's creativity and the belief that every person counts. —Jack Welsh

Now you have the opportunity to make changes to your business with real confidence. You can recognise the qualities and the needs of your change team and identify true leadership styles. You know that making change is an essential part of business growth and that change has to be planned and executed effectively.

*Making Changes Easily* has provided ways to bring about change in small, Medium-sized, and larger organisations or just one division at a time. We have identified pitfalls you may encounter in the beginning of your project and discussed how to prepare for them. There have been explanations, techniques, tools, and tips to support your reviews and revisions during the process of making changes to your business.

You can be confident that you can develop your vision, brainstorm ideas, workshop the best among them, and set effective plans for each stage of your change project. You know how to recover during derailments of your project to put your Change Train[64] back on track and keep the wheels turning. You know how to find your rhythm and keep moving forward with each change idea. There are no limits to making change and making it easily.

One of the greatest experiences you will have when you are making changes will be watching the people around you challenge themselves to achieve the changes you

---

[64] time2manage Change Train Technique®© includes segments about styling the change project development.

have proposed. When they enjoy the changes that they have focused on and achieve their goals, you too are rewarded.

Sometimes it can be the simplest thing that moves you to change. Life is full of choices, and it can be as interesting as you make it, so be as creative as you can when considering your vision for changing your business. Most changes to businesses aim at increasing productivity: whether you're changing the delivery of a product to the market, reducing production costs, or optimising your assets, a change should increase revenue shortly after its implementation.

Norman Vincent Peele said. "Change your thoughts, change your world," So be innovative, show initiative, and ask for assistance if you need it. Be confident that what you want to change is important because you chose it and that you can do it. You have been challenged to go beyond your normal boundaries by considering change, so when you rethink how you do things, you will be taking another step in the change process. You can do it alone or through alliances with others who want to make the same changes in their business. You don't need to be alone in the challenge of change.

Nothing changes if nothing changes. Be bold, be happy, and see how far you can go by working through the process and how you can make changes today. Then give yourself a pat on the back when you arrive at your destination.

The guidelines are included to assist you in making changes easily. When you make a commitment to bring about change, you are on your way to achieving the change. The questions in the guidelines will challenge you to undertake the change you wish to bring about and see the results of your efforts.

# APPENDIX

## Sample Only

Any computer programme that you are using will suffice. This sample is here just to show you what you need to include in an all overview of your month.

(a) Shade or hash out your recreational time first.
(b) Then fill in family time.
(c) Finally, fill in work time schedules. Allow for travel time if you have to travel to meetings so you won't have to rush or be late. Making changes isn't easy, but you will notice an improvement in how you feel when you put yourself first in these schedules.

| Monday

Date: | Tuesday | Wednesday | Thursday | Friday | Saturday | Sunday |
|---|---|---|---|---|---|---|
| | | | | | | |
| | | | | | | |
| | | | | | | |
| | | | | | | |
| | | | | | | |

Notes—Priorities for the month:

_____

_____

_____

_____

_____

_____

_____

_____

## *Sample Action Sheet*

The action list is a vital part of meetings, as it keeps participants from covering the same ground meeting after meeting. Once an action is on the list, it will remain there until completed. The items are numbered, and all tasks are allocated to a participant of the project team until the action is completed.

| Item No. | Item | Start Date | End Date | Responsible Person(s) | Comments, Action Items, Status of Item |
|---|---|---|---|---|---|
| 1 | Team Meeting | … / … | | | |
| | | | | | |
| | | | | | |
| | | | | | |
| | | | | | |

# Meeting Agenda

There are many electronic styles available, but keeping it simple when holding a meeting helps ensure that actions items are assigned to and finalised by a responsible person(s). Meetings should be short, with reading and preparation done beforehand so questions can be asked and answered, and decisions can be made.

| Meeting Agenda | | | |
|---|---|---|---|
| Date: | Time: | | **Type of meeting:** Change Management Proposal |
| Attendees: | | | |
| Preparation required: | | | |
| Please bring: | | | |
| Agenda Items | | | |
| Topic | | Presenter | Time allotted |
| | | | |
| | | | |
| | | | |
| Other information | | | |
| Other Participants: | | | |
| Resources: | | | |

www.ingramcontent.com/pod-product-compliance
Lightning Source LLC
Chambersburg PA
CBHW031837170526
45157CB00001B/336